SWAMI VIVEKANANDA

SWAMI VIVEKANANDA
Excellence in Education

By

Mohit Chakrabarti

GYAN

ISBN : 978-81-783-5479-8

Published, 2018

Published by

Gyan Publishing House
5, Ansari Road
Daryaganj, New Delhi-110002
Phone: 011-47034999, 9811692060
www.gyanbooks.com
E-mail: books@gyanbooks.com

Printed at: G. Print Process, Delhi.

Dedicated to
Professor Yash Pal
Former Chairman
University Grants Commission &
Chairman National Steering Committee
National Curriculum Framework Review
National Council of Educational Research and Training
New Delhi

Contents

Preface

Education is an enquiry of the human mind diverse and infinite. To Swami Vivekananda, it is 'the manifestation of perfection already in man'. It is, as it were, the mirror of the human mind reflecting the vision of the All Beautiful that always awaits revelation in perfumes of promises for greater and more serene possibilities. Apart from the fact that Vivekananda for the first time in the whole history of education has come forward and unfolded the immense power of man as an incomparable exponent of Existence Absolute, Knowledge Absolute and Bliss Absolute, the radical and evolving patterns of education that he has designed for excellence and ascent of man are not only thrilling and pulsating for creative and critical challenges but also vibrant and challenging for education of humane development for all time to come.

Admitting the fact that education is crystallisation of the self from the darkness of ignorance, Vivekananda reminds us that it is the only and surest instrument to wage a relentless war against apathy, hatred, superstition and many more constraints of human progress and civilisation. It is a touchstone of humanism par excellence and most dependable guide to social altruism. At the same time, the introspection of the humans which is essential for aesthetic development together with extinction of personality as the invaluable prize of education is the enviable forte in the educational philosophy of Vivekananda in all poignant resonance in the core of the mind and the heart with mystic resonance.

Religion and education find an altogether new habitation and name in Vivekananda's philosophy of education. Indeed, he makes an adroit synchronisation between the two in the backdrop of humanism, where discipline and an apposite, objective and fool-proof approach to the study of religion as a dynamic force of ascent and excellence of man have been rewarded with priceless dividends.

As regards the relation between education and humanism more often than not mismatched and misinterpreted, Vivekananda for the first time has presented us and generations to come a clear, specific, easily accessible and pulsating panorama of practical methods and contents of studies enriched in oriental heritage and culture well adorned with the erudite ethos and moorings, values and sophistications of erudition and edification of humane endeavour.

With education and social awareness poles apart even today almost anywhere and everywhere, Vivekananda valiantly places the platform of education in the hapless habitations of the poor and the ignorant, the disadvantaged and the downtrodden, the distressed and the devalued, and the lowly and the lost. His clarion call for education in the remotest corners where the wailings of the hungry and the despised are lost in deliberately dumb silence and indifference is yet to be responded in all sincerity and devotion.

Truth, goodness and beauty are not only Vivekananda's ends-in-view of aesthetic education but these are also essential components of man-making and character-building. He reminds us that unless there is an inherent discipline well nurtured in aesthetic education for catholicity of vision and ceaseless refinement of character, education becomes meaningless and useless as it has of late become a veritable burden in the senseless utopia of sham scholarship. The paradise of Sachchidananda as Vivekananda has so hailed and welcomed in the auspicious altar of education can never be lost, lest civilisation right now terribly tainted with super-computerized modernity misses the symphony of simplicity and modesty, austerity and grace, decency and decorum.

In making a perfect cohesion between mysticism and education, perhaps Vivekananda has, besides Rabindranath Tagore, no parallel in the whole history of education for human excellence. Indeed, his very life and work are the eternal path-breakers of how extinction of personality adorns the poignant perfection of man in mystic manifestation. With the vision of Tatohangsa prachodayat in quest of purity and perfection, education awards one with the supreme prize: "I am He (Shivoham)".

I am intensely indebted to Swami Prabhananda, Secretary, The Ramakrishna Mission Institution of Culture, Kolkata I am really very fortunate to work under him as a student-teacher at the Ramakrishna Mission Ashrama, Narendrapur, Kolkata nearly five decades ago. I still recall his vibrant viewpoints and suggestions on the educational philosophy of Swami Vivekananda, which still inspire me to march on in quest of education for excellence.

I am also grateful to Sobdo Chakrabarti, my son, who has assisted me a lot in computer work.

If the book appeals to the educationists, learners and everyone interested in the philosophy of education of Swami Vivekananda in particular, I would definitely feel myself a bit justified as a modest follower and disseminator of meaningful education.

Seemantika **Mohit Chakrabarti**
Seemanto Palli
Santiniketan

1

Education and Aesthetics: Vivekananda's Introspection

Education is an enquiry perennial and thrilling. To Swami Vivekananda, it is more than an enquiry. It is an adventure both internal and external. It is a quest par excellence that cares for decency and decorum of human behaviour both as a social and a divine being. It observes the observer from within in order to be natural and genuine from extrinsic factors and vice versa. It is also a challenge continual and vibrant to be as one ought to be to oneself for well-being of others even at the cost of death.

Vivekananda also penetrates into the world of universal and serene goodness and beauty of man, the best creation, that care for elegance and truth, simplicity and modesty, austerity and sacrifice to the best of abilities and performances. As education is a definite pointer to one's worth in all avenues of life and work, the true pursuer of education always welcomes struggles in diverse and different walks of life, and like a valiant crusader, negotiates all constraints in calmness of mind and sympathy of the heart.

In addition to the aesthetic components of education as above, Vivekananda adroitly draws our attention to the other invaluable components of aesthetics in education for in-depth introspection. In his own words:

Purity is absolutely the basic work, the bed-rock upon which the whole Bhakti-building rests. Cleansing the external body and discriminating the food are both easy, but without internal cleanliness and purity, these external observances are of no value whatsoever. In the list of qualities conducive to purity, as given by Ramanuja, there are enumerated, Satya, truthfulness; Arjava, sincerity; Daya, doing good to others without any gain to one's self; Ahimsa, not injuring others by thought, word, or deed; Anabhidhya, not coveting others' goods, not thinking vain thoughts, and not brooding over injuries received from another. In this list, the one idea that deserves special notice is Ahimsa, non-injury to others. This duty of non-injury is, so to speak, obligatory on us in relation to all things. As with some, it does not simply mean the non-injuring of human beings and mercilessness towards the lower animals; nor, as with some others, does it mean the protecting of cats and dogs and feeding of ants with sugar—with liberty to injure brother-man in every horrible way! It is remarkable that almost every good idea in this world can be carried to a disgusting extreme. A good practice carried to an extreme and worked in accordance with the letter of the law becomes a positive evil.

—Swami Vivekananda: *The Complete Works of Swami Vivekananda*, Advaita Ashrama, Calcutta, Mayavati Memorial Edition, 1989, Vol. III, p. 67.

The education of goodness for one and all is one of the most significant contributions to development of aesthetics inherent in every human being. Vivekananda emphasises on harbouring and cultivating goodness as the aesthetic component because it leads to elimination of hatred and victory of love. It is also the guiding force of nurturing humility which is another vital aesthetic component for fullness in education. In considering such an emancipation of man, his poignant words are very significant:

It is the screen that hides the Self, which is unchanging. The screen opens, and we find the Self behind it. All change is in the screen. In the saint the screen is thin, and the reality can almost shine through. In the sinner, the screen is thick, and we are liable to lose sight of the truth that the Atman is there, as well as behind the saint's screen. When the screen is wholly removed, we find it really never existed—that we were the Atman and nothing else, even the screen is forgotten.

The two phases of this distinction in life are—first, that the man who knows the real Self, will not be affected by anything; secondly, that that man alone can do good to the world. That man alone will have seen the real motive of doing good to others, because there is only one, it cannot be called egoistic, because that would be differentiation. It is the only selflessness. It is the perception of the universal, not of the individual. Every case of love and sympathy is an assertion of this universal. "Not I, but thou". Help another because you are in him and he is in you, is the philosophical way of putting it. The real Vedantist will alone give up his life for a fellow-man without any compunction, because he knows he will not die. As long as there is one insect left in the world, he is living; as long as one mouth eats, he eats. So he goes on doing good to others; and he is never hindered by the modern ideas of caring for the body. When a man reaches this point of abnegation, he goes beyond the moral struggle, beyond everything. He sees in the most learned priest, in the cow, in the dog, in the most miserable places, neither the learned man, nor the cow, nor the dog, nor the miserable place, but the same divinity manifesting itself in them all. He alone is the happy man; and the man who has acquired that sameness has, even in this life, conquered all existence.

—*Ibid.*, Vol. V, pp. 284-285.

Realisation of truth by means of aesthetic manifestation of divinity is the core of Vivekananda's philosophy of education. He draws our attention to the education of sameness of divinity in all including the keen kinship with the world. This is why he places education as an assured means of understanding the real nature of good and evil which are interrelated. With this lesson of aesthetic realisation, truth becomes effulgent, and the person who practises and attains truth out of both good and evil becomes an eternal connoisseur of living goodness.

As a pioneer in the teaching the Vedanta philosophy, Vivekananda poignantly unfolds the aesthetic vision of man in the scanner of good and evil, which ultimately upholds education that compliments with man as the embodiment of 'living blessing':

It is a lie to say that I am a man or a woman, or to say that I belong to this country or that. All the world is my country, the whole universe is mine, because I have clothed myself with it as my body. Yet we see that there are people in this world who are ready to assert these doctrines, and at the same time do things which we should call filthy; and if we ask them why they do so, they tell us that it is our delusion and that they can do nothing wrong. What is the test by which they are to be judged? The test is here.

Though good and evil are both conditioned manifestations of the soul, yet evil is the most external coating, and good is the nearer coating of the real man, the Self. And unless a man cuts through the layer of evil he cannot reach the layer of good, and unless he has passed through both the layers of good and evil he cannot reach the Self. He who reaches the Self, what remains attached to him? A little Karma, a little bit of the momentum of past life, but it is all good momentum. Until the bad momentum is entirely worked out and past impurities are entirely burnt, it is impossible for any man to see and realise truth. So, what is left attached to the man who has reached the Self and seen the truth is the remnant of the good impressions of past life, the good momentum. Even if he lives in the body and works incessantly, he works only to do good; his lips speak only benediction to all; his hands do only good works; his mind can only think good thoughts; his presence is a blessing wherever he goes. He is himself a living blessing. Such a man will, by his very presence, change even the most wicked persons into saints. Even if he does not speak, his very presence will be a blessing to mankind. Can such men do any evil; can they do wicked deeds? There is, you must remember, all the difference of pole to pole between realisation and mere talking. Any fool can talk. Even parrots talk. Talking is one thing, and realising is another. Philosophies, and doctrines, and arguments, and books, and theories, and churches, and sects, and all these things are good in their own way; but when that realisation comes, these things drop away. For instance, maps are good, but when you see the country itself, and look again at the maps, what a great difference you find! So those that have realised truth do not require the ratiocinations of logic and all other gymnastics of the intellect to make them understand the truth; it is to them the life of their lives, concretised, made more than tangible.

—*Ibid.*, II, pp. 283-284.

Education, to be truly aesthetic, must make a symphony of existence, knowledge and bliss. The very existence of man is dependent on how knowledge is pursued. Again, whatever knowledge is pursued and exercised must be a repository of the eternal fountain of joy that is the bliss of education. This union of existence, knowledge and joy is what Vivekananda identifies as the core of the Vedanta philosophy that should be the essential guide to nurturing aesthetics in education. His own explanation on this point is significant:

> The phrase Sat-Chit-Ananda means—Sat, i.e. existence, Chit, i.e. consciousness of knowledge, and Ananda, i.e. bliss which is the same as love. There is no controversy between the Bhakta and the Jnani regarding the Sat aspect of Brahman. Only the Jnanis lay greater stress on His aspect of Chit or knowledge, while the Bhaktas keep the aspect of Ananda or love more in view. But no sooner is the essence of Chit realised than the essence of Ananda is also realised. Because what is Chit is verily the same as Ananda.
>
> —*Ibid.*, Vol. V, p. 385.

The education of aesthetics through identification and assimilation of existence, knowledge and bliss that Vivekananda stimulates us to pursue with devotion and dedication has its closest relation to truth as a great aesthetic force. The man-God-man sameness of relationship based on the education of the aesthetics of truth as he advocates is the guiding principle of humanism for time immemorial:

> I have done my duty to my people fairly well. Now for the world that gave me this body—the country that gave me the ideas, the humanity which allows me to be one of them!

The older I grow, the more I see behind the idea of the Hindus that man is the greatest of all beings. So say the Mohammedans too. The angels were asked by Allah to bow down to Adam. Iblis did not, and therefore he became Satan. This earth is higher than all heavens; this is the greatest school in the universe; and the Mars or Jupiter people cannot be greater than we, because they cannot communicate with us. The only so-called higher beings are the departed, and these are nothing but men who have taken another body. This is finer, it is true, but still a man-body, with hands and feet, and so on. And they live on this earth in another Akasha, without being absolutely invisible. They also think, and have consciousness, and everything else like us. So they also are men, so are the Devas, the angels. But man alone becomes God; and they all have to become men again in order to become God.

—*Ibid.*, pp.93-94.

Vivekananda also marks a new avenue of aesthetics in morality, which he designs and elaborates in education where knowledge breaks the conventional barriers to understanding and appreciating the true concept of religion. He lifts education from toeing with materialisation and scans morality in terms of aesthetics. As such, he makes inroads to morality in introducing freedom of knowledge that enables morality to have its vibrant role in the desirable and spontaneous expansion of the aesthetic man. In his own inimitable words:

In the internal world, each thought is trying to go beyond control. Again each particle in the external world is checked by another force, the centripetal, and drawn towards the centre. Similarly in the thought-world the controlling power is checking all these outgoing desires.

Desires of materialisation, that is, being dragged down more and more to the plane of mechanical action, belong to the animal man. It is only when the desire to prevent all such bondage to the senses arises that religion dawns in the heart of man. Thus we see that the whole scope of religion is to prevent man from falling into the bondage of the senses and to help him to assert his freedom. The first effort of this power of Nivritti towards that end is called morality. The scope of all morality is to prevent this degradation and break this bondage. All morality can be divided into the positive and the negative elements; it says either "Do this" or "Do not do this". When it says, "Do not", it is evident that it is a check to a certain desire which would make a man a slave. When it says, "Do", its scope is to show the way to freedom and to the breaking down of a certain degradation which has already seized the human heart.

Now this morality is only possible if there be a liberty to be attained by man. Apart from the question of the chances of attaining perfect liberty, it is clear that the whole universe is a case of struggle to expand, or in other words, to attain liberty. This infinite space is not sufficient for even one atom. The struggle for expansion must go on eternally until perfect liberty is attained. It cannot be said that this struggle to gain freedom is to avoid pain and to attain pleasure. The lowest grade of beings, who can have no such feeling, are also struggling for expansion; and according to many, man himself is the expansion of these very beings.

—*Ibid.*, Vol. VIII, pp. 146-147.

What type of education for aesthetic advancement can be received from the teacher? What actually should be the role of a teacher in imparting such education? What should be the actual relationship between the teacher and the taught? In response to all these and allied questions, Vivekananda presents an altogether new vision which has practically no parallel in the whole history of education. In fact, a striking relationship between the teacher and the taught as he describes from his own aesthetic experience as a taught turned into a teacher, son, daughter, father etc. by his own master Shri Ramakrishna unfolds a new chapter of the aesthetics of education:

The teacher is not a man who comes just to teach me, and I pay him so much, and there it ends. In India it is really like an adoption. The teacher is more than my own father, and I am truly his child, his son in every respect. I owe him obedience and reverence first, before my own father even; because, they say, the father gave me this body, but he showed me the way to salvation, he is greater than father. And we carry this love, this respect for our teacher all our lives. And this is the only organisation that exists. I adopt my disciples. Sometimes the teacher will be a young man and the disciple a very old man. But never mind, he is the son, and he calls me "Father", and I have to address him as my son, my daughter, and so on.

Now, I happened to get an old man to teach me, and he was very peculiar. He did not go much for intellectual scholarship, scarcely studied books; but when he was a boy he was seized with the tremendous idea of getting truth direct. First, he tried by studying his own religion. Then he got the idea that he must get the truth of other religions; and with that idea he joined all the sects, one after another. For the time being he did exactly what they told him to do—lived with the devotees of these different sects in turn, until interpenetrated with the particular ideal of that sect. After a few years he would go to another sect. When he had gone through with all that, he came to the conclusion that they were all good. He had no criticism to offer to any one; they are all so many paths leading to the same goal. And then he said, "That is a glorious thing, that there should be so many paths, because if there were only one path, perhaps it would suit only an individual man. The more the number of paths, the more the chance for every one of us to know the truth. If I cannot be taught in one language, I will try another, and so on".

—*Ibid.*, pp. 78-79.

The purity of aesthetic education in a broadened vision and wider outlook as Vivekananda has described above has also its serene canvas in the belief in sameness of mind striving for perfection as opposed to mere humility. As a matter of fact, the lesson of truth as one of the most vital components of aesthetic education not only penetrates into the inner world of a being but also shows the avenues of different endeavours of human progress in unfolding perfection in the challenges of infinity. At the same time, such a lesson should always do away with thrusting anything authoritatively. Freedom to accept truth through individual assessment opens the doors of aesthetics in its true entirety. In the words of Vivekananda:

With all my respects for the Rishis of yore, I cannot but denounce their method in instructing the people. They always enjoined upon them to do certain things but took care never to explain to them the reason for it. This method was pernicious to the very core; and instead of enabling them to attain the end, it laid upon their shoulders a mass of meaningless nonsense. Their excuse for keeping the end hidden from view was that the people could not have understood their real meaning even if they had presented it to them, not being worthy recipients. The Adhikarvada is the outcome of pure selfishness. They know that by this enlightenment on their special subject they would lose their superior positions of instructors to the people. Hence their endeavour to support this theory. If you consider a man too weak to receive these lessons, you should try the more to teach and educate him; you should give him the advantage of more coaching, instead of less, to train up his intellect, so as to enable him to comprehend the more subtle problems. These advocates of Adhikarvada ignored the tremendous fact of the infinite possibilities of the human soul. Every man is capable of receiving knowledge if it is imparted in his own language. A teacher who cannot convince others should weep on account of his own inability to teach the people in their own language, instead of cursing them and dooming them to live in ignorance and superstition, setting up the plea that the higher knowledge is not for them. Speak out the truth boldly, without any fear that it will puzzle the weak. Men are selfish; they do not want others to come up to the same level of their knowledge, for fear of losing their own privilege and prestige over others.

—*Ibid.*, Vol. V, pp. 262-263.

Identification with the unchangeable Self within everyone is the key to opening the doors of aesthetic illumination. Vivekananda advocates education for that fullness of vision in aesthetics. This would enable us to identify, control and crystallise our sense-organs by means of education of the highest order that eliminates all worldly temptations and enriches us with the aesthetic grandeur of altruism. As he serenely observes:

The seer is really the Self, the pure one, the ever body, the infinite, the immortal. This is the Self of man. And what are the instruments? The Chitta or mind-stuff, the Buddhi or determinative faculty, the Manas or mind, and the Indriyas or sense-organs. These are the instruments for him to see the external world, and the identification of the Self with the instruments is what is called the ignorance of egoism. We say, "I am the mind", "I am thought", "I am angry", and "I am happy". How can we be angry and how can we hate? We should identify ourselves with the Self that cannot change. If It is unchangeable, how can It be one moment happy, and one moment unhappy? It is formless, infinite, omnipresent. What can change It? It is beyond all law. What can affect It? Nothing in the world can produce an effect on It. Yet through ignorance, we identify ourselves with the mind-stuff, and think we feel pleasure and pain.

—*Ibid.*, Vol. I, pp. 238-239.

Just as elimination of egoism is one of the greatest lessons in Vivekananda's educational philosophy of aesthetics, so is the intense desire to be free from both pleasure and pain, happiness and sorrow—an aesthetic lesson on education of ascent in excellence. This is Mumukshatva or freedom from all temptations, a great aesthetic component that illuminates the inherent divinity in man. Education enriched with this component ennobles the glory of man. Vivekananda exposes this mumukshatva in terms of concrete and transparent day-to-day affairs of life as follows:

When we are healthy, and young, we think that all the wealth of the world will be ours, and when later we get kicked about by society like footballs and get older, we sit in a corner and croak and throw cold water on the enthusiasm of others. Few men know that with pleasure there is pain, and with pain, pleasure; and as pain is disgusting, so is pleasure, as it is the twin brother of pain. It is derogatory to the glory of man that he should be going after pain, and equally derogatory, that he should be going after pleasure. Both should be turned aside by men whose reason is balanced. Why will not men seek freedom from being played upon? This moment we are whipped, and when we begin to weep, nature gives us a dollar; again we are whipped, and when we weep, nature gives us a piece of ginger-bread, and we begin to laugh again.

The sage wants liberty; he finds that sense-objects are all vain and that there is no end to pleasures and pains. How many rich people in the world want to find fresh pleasures! All pleasures are old, and they want new ones. Do you not see how many foolish things they are inventing every day, just to titillate the nerves for a moment, and that done, how there comes a reaction? The majority of people are just like a flock of sheep. If the leading sheep falls into a ditch, all the rest follow and break their necks. In the same way, what one leading member of a society does, all others do, without thinking what they are doing. When a man begins to see the vanity of worldly things, he will feel he ought not to be thus played upon or borne along by nature. That is slavery. If a man has a few kind words said to him, he begins to smile, and when he hears a few harsh words, he begins to weep. He is a slave to a bit of bread, to a breath of air; a slave to dress, a slave to patriotism, to country, to name, and to fame. He is thus in the midst of slavery and the real man has become buried within, through his bondage. What you call man is a slave. When one realises all this slavery, then comes the desire to be free; an intense desire comes. If a piece of burning coal be placed on a man's head, see how he struggles to throw it off. Similar would be the struggles for freedom of a man who really understands that he is a slave of nature.

—*Ibid.*, pp. 410-411.

The education of aesthetics in learning and idealising man as the living God is a pioneering contribution of Vivekananda as an educational philosopher. Unlike others who are more interested in education as an intellectual exercise only, he unfolds a new chapter of aesthetics in the education of religion, where the vision of the Lord is reflected in all the stages of the life of man. Thus the serene aesthetic bond of relationship between God and man makes the perfect unison of intellect and ascent as opposed to dissociation of divinity within. Vivekananda characteristically elucidates:

I shall call you religious from the day you begin to see God in men and women, and then you will understand what is meant by turning the left cheek to the man who strikes you on the right. When you see man as God, everything, even the tiger, will be welcome. Whatever comes to you is but the Lord, the Eternal, the Blessed One, appearing to us in various forms, as our father, and mother, and friend, and child—they are our own soul playing with us.

As our human relationships can thus be made divine, so our relationship with God may take any of these forms and we can look upon Him as our father, or mother, or friend, or beloved. Calling God Mother is a higher ideal than calling Him Father; and to call Him Friend is still higher; but the highest is to regard Him as the Beloved. The highest point of all is to see no difference between lover and beloved. You may remember, perhaps, the old Persian story of how a lover came and knocked at the door of the beloved and was asked, "Who are you?" he answered, "It is I", and there was no response. A second time he came, and exclaimed, "I am here", but the door was not opened. The third time he came, and the voice asked from inside, "Who is there?" He replied, "I am thyself, my beloved", and the door opened. So is the relation between God and ourselves. He is everything. Every man and woman is the palpable, blissful, living God. Who says God is unknown? Who says He is the searched after? We have found God eternally. We have been living in Him eternally; everywhere He is eternally known, eternally worshipped.

—*Ibid.*, Vol. V, pp. 326-327.

Extinction of personality is one of the most desirable aesthetic sensibilities that everyone should strive through education. Vivekananda shows the most common avenue of such a striving with, of course, finer moderation. His strategy is to work for the exercise of knowledge that leads to liberation from all worldly desires which must precede before any work. Work for the sake of work leads to nothing, education notwithstanding. This is why he stresses on making a ceaseless endeavour to visualise the inner light through knowledge before any work to be undertaken for execution. Meanwhile, with sincerity as the aesthetic component of both knowledge and work, education for seeking the science of the Maker as Vivekananda identifies God becomes meaningful and worthwhile. In his own words:

To attain liberation through work, join yourself to work but without desire, looking for no result. Such work leads to knowledge, which in turn brings emancipation. To give up work before you know, leads to misery. Work done for the Self gives no bondage. Neither desire pleasure nor fear pain from work. It is the mind and the body that work, not I. Tell yourself this unceasingly and realise it. Try not to know that you work.

Do all as a sacrifice or offering to the Lord. Be in the world, but not of it, like the lotus leaf whose roots are in the mud but which remains always pure. Let your love go to all, whatever they do to you. A blind man cannot see colour, so how can we see evil unless it is in us? We compare what we see outside with what we see in ourselves and pronounce judgment accordingly. If we are pure, we cannot see impurity. It may exist, but not for us. See only God in every man, woman and child; see it by the antarjyotis, "inner light", and seeing that, we can see naught else. Do not want this world, because what you desire you get. Seek the Lord and the Lord only. The more power there is, the more bondage, the more fear. How much more afraid and miserable are we than the ant! Get out of it all and come to the Lord. Seek the science of the maker and not that of the made.

—*Ibid.*, Vol. VII, pp. 63-64.

A ceaseless pursuit for the science of the maker not in artificiality but with a genuine sense of involvement is, as Vivekananda reminds us, the hallmark of exercise in aesthetic education. Purity in thought and action, sincerity in performance and dedication are the lessons which must be evolved out of one's own response within and not from an external source as the Lord is inherent and omnipresent. One cannot evade this truth by any means.

Vivekananda goes a step further in aesthetic education in making us responsible for unfolding the Lord within in education that cares for fullness in aesthetic education. The task is undeniably very difficult but definitely very challenging. The cup of life assigned to us is a beckoning of the long and arduous journey to win over passion and crystallise contemplation disciplined in decency and transparency beyond joy, beyond grace. Why not make a grand celebration of inner aesthetic consciousness by reciting the kindred and poignant words as Vivekananda has written in his poem "The Cup"?

This is your cup—the cup assigned to you from the beginning,

Nay, My child, I know how much of that dark drink is your own brew

Of fault and passion, ages long ago,

In the deep years of yesterday, I know.

This is your road—a painful road and drear.

I made the stones that never give you rest.

I set your friend in pleasant ways and clear,

And he shall come like you, unto My breast.

But you, My child, must travel here.

This is your task. It has no joy nor grace,

But it is not meant for any other hand,

And in My universe hath measured place,

Take it. I do not bid you understand.

I bid you close your eyes to see My face.

—*Ibid.*, Vol. VI, p. 177.

2

Education and Mysticism: Vivekananda's March for Excellence

Education is to bring about a change in oneself. It is a continual endeavour for the desirable change of consciousness. It is a discipline in the inherent system to be exercised with all precision and propriety. It creates doubts and distortions only to find newer avenues of marching ahead.

To Vivekananda, education is more than marching ahead. It is marching beyond what one thinks and acts in course of continuous endeavour. The components that enable one to do so are the finer qualities of the head and the heart—humility, strength, truth, compassion, sympathy, care, courage, devotion, sacrifice and service, to name a few. But what acts as the driving force of all is advancing beyond the range of consciousness, which paves for the enrichment of the inner self to be enlightened with the effulgence of inherent divinity—an endless adventure into the serene world of mysticism.

The poignancy and penetrating vision of education for mystic fulfilment are the touchstones of understanding and appreciating divinity. It is a passion beyond passion, an attraction crystallised by controlled emotional sensibilities. It does not allow impure thoughts to thrive in the unusual ukase of sentimentalism. It is a continual and disciplined training of how to exceed veritable consciousness to accelerate freedom for winning over all constraints material or mental whatsoever or howsoever. The first lesson of education for mystic advancement, therefore, is to unendingly strive for visualising the All Beautiful anywhere and everywhere above everyone and everything. Vivekananda adroitly enumerates on this point.

If we are ever to gain freedom, it must be by conquering nature, never by running away. Cowards never win victories. We have to fight fear and troubles and ignorance if we expect them to flee before us.

What is death? What are terrors? Do you not see the Lord's face in them? Fly from evil and terror and misery, and they will follow you. Face them, and they will flee. The whole world worships ease and pleasure, and very few dare to worship that which is painful. To rise above both is the idea of freedom. Unless man passes through this gate he cannot be free. We all have to face these. We strive to worship the Lord, but the body rises between Him and us and blinds our vision. We must learn how to worship and love Him in the thunderbolt, in shame, in sorrow, in sin. All the world has ever been preaching the God of virtue. I preach a God of virtue and a God of sin in one. Take Him if you dare—that is the one way to salvation; then alone will come to us the Truth Ultimate which comes from the idea of oneness. Then will be lost the idea that one is greater than another. The nearer we approach the law of freedom, the more we shall come under the Lord, and troubles will vanish. Then we shall not differentiate the door of hell from the gate of heaven, nor differentiate between man and say, "I am greater than any being in the universe." Until we see nothing in the world but the Lord Himself, all these evils will beset us and we shall make all these distinctions; because it is only in the Lord, in the Spirit, that we are all one; and until we see God everywhere, this unity will not exist for us.

—Swami Vivekananda: *The Complete Works of Swami Vivekananda*, Advaita Ashrama, Calcutta, Mayavati Memorial Edition, 1989, Vol. I, p. 339.

The lesson of mystic fulfilment is to reduce oneself to a cipher, never taking interest in either sorrow or happiness, pleasure or pain because all these remain absolutely meaningless for a perfectly balanced mind. Moreover, education for mystic fullness as Vivekananda observes, is possible only when love becomes one of the most significant components of mystic emancipation. In defining and explaining Raja-Yoga, he adroitly brings out this mystic vision:

What is this Raja-Yoga, this controlling of the mind? In this country you are associating all sorts of hobgoblins with the word Yoga, I am afraid. Therefore, I must start by telling you that it has nothing to do such things. No one of these Yogas gives up reason, no one of them asks you to be hoodwinked or to deliver your reason into the hands of priests of any type whatsoever. No one of them asks that you should give your allegiance to any superhuman messenger. Each one of them tells you to cling to your reason to hold fast to it. We find in all beings three sorts of instruments of knowledge. The first is instinct, which you find most highly developed in animals; this is the lowest instrument of knowledge. What is the second instrument of knowledge? Reasoning. You find that most highly developed in man. Now in the first place, instinct is an inadequate instrument; to animals, the sphere of action is very limited, and within that limit instinct acts. When you come to man, you see it is largely developed into reason. The sphere of action also has here become enlarged. Yet even reason is still very insufficient. Reason can go only a little way and then it stops, it cannot go any further; and if you try to push it, the result is helpless confusion, reason itself becomes unreasonable. Logic becomes arguments in a circle. Take, for instance, the very basis of our perception, matter and force. What is matter? That which is acted upon by force. And force? That which acts upon matter. You see the complication, what the logicians call see-saw, one idea developing on the other, and this again depending on that. You find a mighty barrier before reason, beyond which reasoning cannot go; yet it always feels impatient to get into the region of the Infinite beyond, this world, this universe which our senses feel, or our mind thinks, is but one atom, so to say, of the Infinite, projected on to the plane of consciousness; and within that narrow limit, defined by the network of consciousness, works our reason, and not beyond. Therefore, there must be some other instrument to take us beyond, and that instrument is called inspiration. So instinct, reason, and inspiration are the three instruments of knowledge. Instinct belongs to animals, reason to man, and inspiration to God-men. But in all human beings are to be found, in a more or less developed condition, the germs of all these instruments of knowledge. To have these mental instruments evolved, the germs must be there.

—*Ibid.*, Vol. II, pp. 388-390.

The efflorescence of mysticism that Vivekananda has advocated through education has its genesis in harbouring oneself in the mystic world of Sachchidananda which is as he defines, 'Absolute existence and Immortality'. But that promising world of mystic efflorescence pre-determines and pre-supposes an infallible and obligatory exercise in and through education. It is the exercise of boldness. And for this, again, the exercise of truth would strengthen the mission for a sounder and more accessible world of mysticism. Vivekananda categorically observes:

I cannot believe in the self-contradictory statement that light brings greater darkness. It is like losing life in the ocean of Sachchidananda, in the ocean of Absolute existence and Immortality. How absurd! Knowledge means freedom from the errors which ignorance leads to knowledge paying the way to error! Enlightenment leading to confusion! Is it possible? Men are not bold enough to speak out broad truths for fear of losing the respect of the people. They try to make a compromise between the real, eternal truths and the nonsensical prejudices of the people, and thus set up the doctrine that Lokacharas (customs of the people) and Deshacharas (customs of the country) must be adhered to. No compromise! No white-washing! No covering of corpses beneath flowers! Throw away such texts as "Tathapi Lokacharah—yet the customs of the people have to be followed." Nonsense! The result of this sort of compromise is that the grand truths are soon buried under heaps of rubbish, and the latter are eagerly held as real truths. Even the grand truths of the Gita, so boldly preached by Shri Krishna, received the gloss of compromise in the hands of future generations of disciples, and the result is that the grandest picture of the world is now made to yield many things which lead men astray.

This attempt at compromise proceeds from arrant downright cowardice. Be bold! My children should be brave, above all. Not the least compromise on any account. Preach the highest truths broadcast. Do not fear losing your respect or causing unhappy friction. Rest assured that if you serve truth in spite of temptations to forsake it, you will attain a heavenly strength in the face of which men will quail to speak before you things which you do not believe to be true.

People will be convinced of what you will say to them if you can strictly serve truth for fourteen years continually, without swerving from it. Thus you will confer the greatest blessing of the masses, unshackle their bondages, and uplift the whole nation.

—*Ibid.*, Vol. V, pp. 264-265.

To a perfect mystic visionary, education accelerates beyond the domains of both knowledge and intelligence because both are very often identified as a single entity in a human being but fail to coordinate the entire world of education as such and education beyond the range of intelligence and knowledge. That can only be possible when we take recourse the education of the soul—the Purusha—which defies all laws of causation and heralds the true nature of man. That is the only avenue of education for mystic ascent and excellence. Vivekananda exquisitely elucidates on the role of Purusha as an invaluable mystic component in the education for mystic excellence as follows:

We have to believe that we are free, yet at every moment we find we are not free. If one idea is a delusion, the other is also a delusion, and if one is true, the other also is true, because both stand upon the same basis, consciousness. The Yogi says, both are true; that we are bound so far as intelligence goes, that we are free so far as the soul is concerned. It is the real nature of man, the soul, the Purusha, which is beyond all the law of causation. Its freedom is percolating through layers of matter in various forms, intelligence, mind etc. it is its light which is shining through all.

Intelligence has no light of its own. Each organ has a particular centre in the brain; it is not that all the organs have one centre; each organ is separate. Why do all perceptions harmonise? Where do they get their unity? If it were in the brain, it would be necessary for all the organs, the eyes, the nose, the ears, etc., to have one centre only, while we know for certain that there are different centres for each. Both a man can see and hear at the same time, so a unity must be there at the back of intelligence. Intelligence is connected with the brain, but behind intelligence even stands the Purusha, the unit, where different sensations and perceptions join and become one. The soul itself is the centre where all the different perceptions converge and become unified. That soul is free, and it is its freedom that tells you every moment that you are free. But you mistake, and mingle that freedom every moment with intelligence and mind. You try to attribute that freedom to the intelligence, and immediately find that intelligence is not free; you attribute that freedom to the body, and immediately nature tells you that you are again mistaken. That is why there is this mingled sense of freedom and bondage at the same time.

—*Ibid.*, Vol. I, pp. 254-255.

The mystic lesson of joy that Vivekananda highlights in his philosophy of education is a penetrating and challenging process of altruism. The emphasis he primarily gives in the learning and appreciating such education for mystic fullness is to be an eternal follower of truth. In doing so there must be a three-fold endeavour: first, visualising oneself as an infinite being always striving for what is beyond from what is within, second, realising the great truth that in worldly sensibilities there are pleasures and pain, sorrow and happiness, fear and temptations, hatred and love, which must be won by the great vision of Oneness which shows the emancipation of 'I' from all sham reality, and third, the power to accept all the responsibilities of others in oneself for the eternal truth that goes beyond knowledge and makes the many as One which is the vision of the ever majestic All Beyond.

Admittedly, Vivekananda expands the mystic aroma of education in the perfume of Oneness. Explaining the Advaitist philosophy of man, he unfolds the relation between man as the 'Infinite Being of the universe' and man beyond all life and all death. In his own words:

Illusion arises from illusion alone. There will be no illusion as soon as the truth is seen. Illusion always rests upon illusion; it never rests upon God, the Truth, the Atman. You are never in illusion; it is illusion that is in you, before you. A cloud is here; another comes and pushes it aside and takes its place. Still another comes and pushes that one away. As before the eternal blue sky, clouds of various hue and colour come, remain for a short time and disappear, leaving it the same eternal blue, even so are you, eternally pure, eternally perfect. You are the veritable Gods of the universe; nay, there are not two, there is but One. It is a mistake to say, "you and I"; say "I". It is I who am eating in millions of mouths; how can I be hungry? It is I who am working through an infinite number of hands; how can I be inactive? It is I who am living the life of the whole universe; where is death for me? I am beyond all life, beyond all death. Where shall I seek for freedom? I am free by my nature. Who can bind me—the God of this universe? The scriptures of the world are but little maps, wanting to delineate my glory, who am the only existence of the universe. Then what are these books to me? Thus says the Advaitist.

"Know the truth and be free in a moment." All the darkness will then vanish. When man has seen himself as one with the Infinite Being of the universe, when all separateness is ceased, when all men and women, all gods and angels, all animals and plants, and the whole universe have melted into that oneness, then all fear disappears. Can I hurt myself? Can I kill myself? Can I injure myself? Whom to fear? Can you fear yourself? Then will all sorrow disappear. What can cause me sorrow? I am the One Existence of the universe. Then all jealousies will disappear; of whom to be jealous? Of myself? Then all bad feelings disappear. Against whom can I have bad feeling? Against myself? There is none in the universe but I. And this is the one way, says the Vedantist, to Knowledge. Kill out the differentiation, kill out this superstition that there are many.

—*Ibid.*, Vol. II, pp.251-252.

The spirit of mysticism serenely married to aesthetics is Vivekananda's forte in education for ascent and excellence. The whole canvas of human society awaits this education for enlightenment of the inner man who knows how to learn the best lesson of introspection and beyond that, where the white lily of freshness and fragrance blooms in incomparable grandeur. As Vivekananda vibrantly advises:

> It is life to do good, it is death not to do good to others. Ninety per cent of human brutes you see are dead, are ghosts—for none lives, my boys, but he who loves. Feel, my children, feel; feel for the poor, the ignorant, the downtrodden; feel till the heart stops and the brain reels and you think you will go mad—then pour the soul out at the feet of the Lord, and then will come power, help, and indomitable energy. Struggle, struggle was my motto for the last ten years. Struggle, still say I. When it was all dark, I used to say, struggle; when light is breaking in, I will say, struggle. Be not afraid, my children. Look not up in that attitude of fear towards that infinite starry vault as if it would crush you. Wait! In a few hours more, the whole of it will be under your feet. Wait, money does not pay, nor name; fame does not pay, nor learning. It is love that pays; it is character that cleaves its way through adamantine walls of difficulties.
>
> —*Ibid.*, Vol. IV, p367.

A broadened vision and a widened outlook are hallmarks of education for mystic awareness. For such education Vivekananda suggests to honour the eternal power to arise and awake for the great sacrifice of the narrow self and illumination of the evolving consciousness for the beyond. It is a preparation serene and sublime for entry and encounter into the void of fullness in devotion and dedication in catholic poignancy. Identifying and elucidating the true nature of the ideal man in terms of education for mystic emancipation, he significantly remarks:

> The ideal man is he who, in the midst of the greatest silence and solitude, finds the intensest activity, and in the midst of the intensest activity finds the silence and solitude of the desert. He has learnt the secret of restraint, he has controlled himself. He goes through the streets of a big city with all its traffic, and his mind is as calm as if he were in a cave, where not a sound could reach him; and he is intensely working all the time. That is the ideal of Karma-Yoga, and if you have attained to that you have really learnt the secret of work.
>
> But we have to begin from the beginning, to take up the works as they come to us and slowly make ourselves more unselfish every day. We must do the work and find out the motive power that prompts us; and, almost without exception, in the first years, we shall find that our motives are always selfish; but gradually this selfishness will melt by persistence, till at last will come the time when we shall be able to do really unselfish work. We may all hope that some day or other, as we struggle through the paths of life, there will come a time when we shall become perfectly unselfish; and the moment that we attain to that, all our powers will be concentrated, and the knowledge which is ours will be manifest.
>
> —*Ibid.*, Vol. I, pp. 34-35.

What, then, should be the end-in-view of a mystic visionary who strives for ascent and excellence? How to have education that shows the way to the Absolute, the way in which every I becomes everything—Existence, Knowledge and Bliss in unison as the All Serene in all? The answers are there in Vivekananda's voice in the translation of Shankaracharya's poem, and its concluding lines are the prelude to the unparalleled marvels of man:

> I have neither death nor fear of death, nor caste;
>
> Nor was I ever born, nor had I parents, friends, and relations;
>
> I have neither Guru, nor disciple;
>
> A am Existence Absolute, Knowledge Absolute, Bliss Absolute—
>
> I am He, I am He. (Shivoham, Shivoham).
>
> I am untouched by the senses, I am neither Mukti nor knowable;
>
> I am without form, without limit, beyond space, beyond time;
>
> I am in everything; I am the basis of the universe; everywhere am I.
>
> I am Existence Absolute, Knowledge Absolute, Bliss Absolute—

I am He, I am He. (Shivoham, Shivoham).

—*Ibid.*, Vol. IV, p. 392.

Are we prepared for such a mystic ascent and excellence in education?

3

Education and Social Awareness: Vivekananda's Synchronisation

Education is always an altruistic activity. To Swami Vivekananda, it becomes really meaningful and worthwhile when it changes each "I" to an ardent "We" in order to be truly social. It is not an easy task. The education of self-preparation for self-surrender to the greater cause of we-ness is always challenging. It welcomes three factors. First, the constraints of the little self is to be overcome not by force external but by the one internal which may be identified as the education of discipline. In this regard, one must be a hard task master within oneself, being, of course, guided by experiences in real life situations. Second, whatever experience one encounters should be looked upon in terms of crystallisation of the self consciously and continually, lest anything detrimental to enrichment of the spirit of altruism must not, under any circumstances, be ignored or affected. Third, the call of the Supreme Self awaiting sincere response and dedication even at the cost of all personal interests of petty pleasure and satisfaction must be adhered to with earnest and untiring devotion and poignancy of perfection. Therefore, the "I-We" sphere of the mental ukase is controlled and replaced by a new education for inner illumination which is the starting point of education for social awareness.

Vivekananda makes inroads to inner awareness for the advancement of social sensibilities in a very distinct, categorical and positive way. He delves deep into the three fundamental forces of nature viz. Sattva or equilibrium, Tamas or inactivity or darkness and Rajas or activity. These are the three forces which require proper social synchronization in the education of every human being. As he characteristically elucidates:

In every man there are these three forces. Sometimes Tamas prevails. We become lazy, we cannot move. We are inactive, bound down by certain ideas or by mere dullness. At other times activity prevails, and at still other times that calm balancing of both. Again, in different men, one of these forces is generally predominant. The characteristic of one man is inactivity, dullness and laziness; that of another, activity, power, manifestation of energy; and in still another we find the sweetness, calmness, and gentleness, which are due to the balancing of both action and inaction. So in all creation—in animals, plants, and men—we find the more or less typical manifestation of all these different forces.

Karma-Yoga has specially to deal with these three factors. By teaching what they are and how to employ them, it helps us to do our work better. Human society is a graded organisation. We all know about morality, and we all know about duty, but at the same time we find that in different countries the significance of morality varies greatly. What is regarded as moral in one country may in another be considered perfectly immoral. For instance, in one country cousins may marry; in another, it is thought to be very immoral; in one, men may marry their sisters-in-law; in another, it is regarded as immoral; in one country people may marry only once; in another, many times; and so forth. Similarly, in all other departments of morality, we find the standard varies greatly—yet we have the idea that there must be a universal standard of morality.

So it is with duty. The idea of duty varies much among different nations. In one country, if a man does not do certain things, people will say he has acted wrongly; while if he does those very things in another country, people will say that he did not act rightly—and yet we know that there must be some universal idea of duty. In the same way, one class of society thinks that certain things are among its duty, while another class thinks quite the opposite and would be horrified if it had to do those things. Two ways are left open to us—the way of the ignorant, who think that there is only one way to truth and that all the rest are wrong, and the way of the wise, who admit that, according to our mental constitution or the different planes of existence in which we are, duty and morality may vary. The important thing is to know that these are gradations of duty and of morality—that the duty of one state of life, in one set of circumstances, will not and cannot be that of another.

—Swami Vivekananda: *The Complete Works of Swami Vivekananda*, Advaita Ashrama, Calcutta, Mayavati Memorial Edition, 1989, Vol. I, pp. 36-37.

The lesson of love as the social outcome of vibrant education that Vivekananda has introduced has its most significant role in transforming our world as a beautiful social platform of awareness. This requires elimination of personal interest, where education serves as a guide to nurture the components of the social self—the self that is always prepared to sacrifice personal interest. Hatred, ill-feeling towards others in the society will, then, be replaced by the spirit of togetherness under the sincere bond of social enlightenment. Vivekananda adroitly highlights on this synchronised spirit of education and social consciousness:

People never stop to think that those who bestowed the least thought on their own individualities have been the greatest workers in the world. Then alone a man loves when he finds that the object of his love is not any low, little, mortal thing. Then alone a man loves when he finds that the object of his love is not a clod on earth, but it is the veritable God Himself. The wife will love the husband the more when she thinks that the husband is God Himself. The husband will love the wife the more when he knows that the wife is

God Himself. The mother will love the children more who thinks that the children are God Himself. That man will love his greatest enemy who knows that that very enemy is God Himself. That man will love a holy man who knows that the holy man is God Himself, and that very man will also love the unholiest of men because he knows the background of that unholiest of men is He, the Lord. Such a man becomes a world-mover for whom his little self is dead and God stands in its place. The whole universe will become transfigured to him. That which is painful and miserable will all vanish; struggles will all depart and go. Instead of being a prison-house, where we everyday struggle and fight and compete for a morsel of bread, this universe will then be to us a playground. Beautiful will be this universe then! Such a man alone has the right to stand up and say, "How beautiful is this world!" he alone has the right to say that it is all good. This will be the great good to the world resulting from such realisation, that instead of this world going on with all its friction and clashing, if all mankind today realise only a bit of that great truth, the aspect of the whole world will be changed, and, in place of fighting and quarrelling, there would be a reign of peace. This indecent and brutal hurry which forces us to go ahead of every one else will then vanish from the world. With it will vanish all struggle, with it will vanish all hate, with it will vanish all jealousy, and all evil will vanish away for ever. Gods will live then upon this earth. This very earth will then become heaven, and what evil can there be when gods are playing with gods, when gods are working with gods, and gods are loving gods? That is the great utility of divine realisation. Everything that you see in society will be changed and transfigured then. No more will you think of man as evil; and that is the first great gain. No more will you stand up and sneeringly cast a glance at a poor man or woman who has made a mistake. No more, ladies, you look down with contempt upon the poor woman who walks the street in the night, because you will see even there God Himself. No more will you think of jealousy and punishments. They will all vanish; and love, the great ideal of love, will be so powerful that no whip and cord will be necessary to guide mankind aright.

—*Ibid.*, Vol. II, pp. 286-287.

The education of the masses as Vivekananda emphasises, denotes how social transformation can be geared towards the right direction of perfection. There cannot be any monopolisation in education and intelligence. Dissemination of education is the only solution for eliminating social evils. The more we would be concerned with the spirit of education for all, the more will be our dividends in social transparencies. In a letter addressed to Shrimati Sarala Ghosal, Editor, Bharati, from Darjeeling on 24 April 1897, Vivekananda writes:

From the day when education and culture etc. began to spread gradually from patricians to plebeians, grew the distinction between the modern civilisation as of Western countries, and the ancient civilisation as of India, Egypt, Rome, etc. I see it before my eyes, a nation is advanced in proportion as education and intelligence spread among the masses. The chief cause of India's ruin has been the monopolising of the whole education and intelligence of the land, by dint of pride and royal authority, among a handful of men. If we are to rise again, we shall have to do it in the same way, i.e. by spreading education among the masses.

—*Ibid.*, Vol. IV, p. 482.

Even education for spiritual development demands cultivation among the masses and should not be limited to the isolated and advantaged few. Accordingly, the masses in the entire society should be imparted the education of their spiritual development. Care should be taken to see that all lessons on spiritual excellence should be oriented towards better ascent of the society in all directions of human endeavour. It should also cater to the needs of eliminating all inconsistencies in spiritual exercise through education of tolerance and sympathy which act as pillars to the success of unambiguous and crystallised spiritual development. When Vivekananda takes recourse to the study of Sanskrit for this purpose of perfection in socio-spiritual education, he has at least three-fold end-in-view of education. First, as a social being, every person undergoing spiritual exercise in education would be able to think seriously of the well-being of the society first in lieu of thinking and learning for self-satisfaction and self-fulfilment only. Second, the spirit of the society as a platform of conjoint spiritual exercise in education for decent living becomes meaningful and evident. Third, the tradition, culture and heritage of the ancient socio-spiritual glory and advancement in education serve as a strong foundation of education of the society, by the society and for the society. But, as these necessitate proper and easily accessible language of communication in the most functional and arresting way, the task of the teacher is to take recourse to simplicity of understanding and appreciation through the mother tongue. Vivekananda's own words on this point are very significant:

My idea is first of all to bring out the gems of spirituality that are stored up in our books and in the possession of a few only, hidden, as it were, in monasteries and in forests—to bring them out; to bring the knowledge out of them, not only from the hands where it is hidden, but from the still more inaccessible chest, the language in which it is preserved, the incrustation of centuries of Sanskrit words. In one word, I want to make them popular. I want to bring out these ideas and let them be the common property of all, of every man in India, whether he knows the Sanskrit language or not. The great difficulty in the way is the Sanskrit language—the glorious language of ours; and this difficulty cannot be removed until—if it is possible—the whole of our nation are good Sanskrit scholars. You will understand the difficulty when I tell you that I have been studying this language all my life, and yet every new book is new to me. How much more difficult would it then be for people who never had time to study the language thoroughly! Therefore the ideas must be taught in the language of people; at the same time, Sanskrit education must go on along with it, because the very sound of Sanskrit words gives a prestige and a power and a strength to the race. The attempts of the great Ramanuja and of Chaitanya and of Kabir to raise the lower classes of India show that marvellous results were attained during the lifetime of those great prophets; yet the later failures will have to be explained, and cause shown why the effect of their teachings stopped within a century of the passing away of these great Masters. The secret is here. They raised the lower classes; they had all the wish that these should come up, but they did not apply their energies to the spreading of the Sanskrit language among the masses.

—*Ibid.*, Vol. III, pp.290-291.

That knowledge without culture among the masses makes education meaningless and a failure necessitates the right organisation and dissemination with the introduction of mother tongue. At the same time, quickness in learning results only when the hoi polloi are honoured with mass participation in education. As Vivekananda explains:

Knowledge came, but the prestige was not there, culture was not there. It is culture that withstands shocks, not a simple mass of knowledge. You can put a mass of knowledge into the world, but that will not do it much good. There must be culture into the blood. We all know in modern times of nations which have masses of knowledge, but what of them? They are like tigers, they are like savages, because culture is not there. Knowledge is only skin-deep, as civilisation is, and a little scratch brings out the old savage. Such things happen; this is the danger. Teach the masses in the vernaculars, give them ideas; they will get information, but something more is necessary; give them culture. Until you give them that, there can be no permanence in the raised condition of the masses.

—*Ibid.*, p. 291.

The quest for the real nature of man has its ultimate success in understanding the limitations of knowledge that fails to be free from egoism. Vivekananda always encourages the pursuit of education that teaches the lesson of self-abnegation and welcomes altruism under any circumstances. Therefore, the ultimate goal of education for social welfare is to rise above selfishness and prepare for any form of sacrifice which leads to social goodness. While explaining the true identity of knowledge in education, Vivekananda exquisitely unfolds this truth:

Knowledge is a limitation, knowledge is objectifying. He is the eternal subject of anything, the eternal witness in this universe, your own Self. Knowledge is, as it were, a lower step, a degeneration. We are that eternal subject already; how can we know it? It is the real nature of every man, and he is struggling to express it in various ways; otherwise, why are there so many ethical codes? Where is the explanation of all ethics? One idea stands out as the centre of all ethical systems, expressed in various forms, namely, doing good to others. The guiding motive of mankind should be charity towards men, charity towards all animals. But these are all various expressions of that eternal truth that "I am the universe; this universe is one". Or else, where is the reason? Why should I do good to my fellowmen? Why should I do good to others? What compels me? It is sympathy, the feeling of sameness everywhere. The hardest hearts feel sympathy for other beings sometimes. Even the man who gets frightened if he is told that this assumed individuality is really a delusion that it is ignoble to try to cling to this apparent individuality; that very man will tell you that extreme of self-abnegation is the centre of all morality. And what is perfect self-abnegation? It means the abnegation of this apparent Self, the abnegation of all selfishness. This idea of "me and mine"—Ahamkara and Mamata–is the result of past superstition, and the more this present self passes away, the more the real Self becomes manifest. This is true self-abnegation, the centre, the basis, the gist of all moral teaching; and whether man knows it or not, the whole world is slowly going towards it, practising it more or less. Only, the vast majority of mankind are doing it unconsciously. Let them do it consciously. Let them make the sacrifice, knowing that this "me and mine" is not the real Self, but only a limitation. But one glimpse of that infinite reality which is behind—but one spark of that infinite fire that is the All—represents the present man; the Infinite is his true nature.

—*Ibid.*, Vol. II, pp. 82-83.

The development of an individual by means of introducing education for the welfare of others is the touchstone of social advancement. Vivekananda goes a step further in incorporating the components of integrity, sympathy and love—the three milestones of education for social consciousness. The creation of educational institutions for exercise of these essential components of humane development can alone guarantee a nation's progress. As he categorically suggests:

All healthy social changes are the manifestations of the spiritual forces working within, and if these are strong and well adjusted, society will arrange itself accordingly. Each individual has to work out his own salvation; there is no other way, and so also with nations. Again, the great institutions of every nation are the conditions of its very existence and cannot be transformed by the mould of any other race. Until higher institutions have been evolved, any attempt to break the old ones will be disastrous. Growth is always gradual.

It is very easy to point out the defects of institutions, all being more or less imperfect, but he is the real benefactor of humanity who helps the individual to overcome the imperfections under whatever institutions he may live. The individuals being raised, the nation and its institutions are bound to rise. But customs and laws are ignored by the virtuous, and unwritten but mightier laws of love, sympathy, and integrity take their place. Happy is the nation which can rise to the necessity of but few law books, and needs no longer to bother its head about this or that institution. Good men rise beyond all laws, and will help their fellows to rise under whatever conditions they live.

—*Ibid.*, Vol. V, pp. 415-416.

Education for regeneration of India as Vivekananda has visualised and practised must be rooted to the masses. Unless education of the masses is prioritised, the dream of a socially enlightened India will always remain unfulfilled. In an interview with the representative of the Madras Times in February 1897, he has invaluably disclosed his intention on this point:

I consider that the great national sin is the neglect of the masses, and that is one of the causes of our downfall. No amount of politics would be of any avail until the masses of India are once more well educated, well fed, and well cared for. They pay for our education, they build our temples, but in return they get kicks. They are practically our slaves. If we want to regenerate India, we must work for them. I want to start two central institutions at first—one at Madras and the other at Calcutta—for training young men as preachers. I have funds for starting the Calcutta one. English people will find funds for my purpose.

My faith is in the younger generation, the modern generation, out of them will come my workers. They will work out the whole problem, like lions. I have formulated the idea, and I have given my life to it. If I do not achieve success, some better one will come after me to work it out, and I shall be content to struggle.

—*Ibid.*, pp. 222-223.

The education of love as Vivekananda observes, is the fundamental driving force for social unison and social advancement. It serves as a law of life that indicates hope for a better society to live in peace and prosperity. It becomes more than education in the ordinary meaning of life that is always afraid of struggle, destruction and death. Vivekananda advises us not to be dwarfed by constraints but, on the other hand, accept all social challenges with strong determination and undaunted resolution for love and goodness, welfare and benevolence for the poor and downtrodden, the ignored and despised in the society. His vibrant message to Alasinga Perumal on 19 November 1894 from New York in this connection is very significant:

Nothing else is necessary but these—love, sincerity and patience. What is life but growth, i.e. expansion i.e. love? Therefore all love is life, it is the only law of life; all selfishness is death, and this is true here or hereafter. It is life to do good, it is death not to do good to others. Ninety per cent of human brutes you see are dead, are ghosts—for none lives, my boys, but he who loves. Feel, my children, feel; feel for the poor, the ignorant, the downtrodden; feel till the heart stops and the brain reels and you think you will go mad—then pour the soul out at the feet of the Lord, and then will come power, help, and indomitable energy. Struggle, struggle was my motto for the last ten years. Struggle, still say I. When it was all dark, I used to say, struggle; when light is breaking in, I still say, struggle. Be not afraid, my children. Look not up in that attitude of fear towards that infinite starry vault as if it would crush you. Wait! In a few hours more, the whole of it will be under your feet. Wait, money does not pay, nor name; fame does not pay, nor learning. It is love that pays; it is character that cleaves its way through adamantine walls of difficulties.

—*Ibid.*, Vol. IV, p. 367.

For the lesson of education to be truly social, love, indeed, is the most assured and dependable component. Vivekananda refers to the children of Japan who have the natural and instinctive love for dolls, and, as such, they never break their dolls. Why do they love even an inanimate thing like a doll? The reason is clear and worth emulation. They love dolls because they do believe that their love would make these animated. Unless this living spirit of love for the people of the society is a vibrant lesson in practice in the sphere of education, the purpose of education for an enlightened and humane society is bound to be crushingly defeated. Vivekananda deliberates upon the matter in a very pointed and crystallised way:

Everyone has the power to judge of good and evil, but he is the hero who undaunted by the waves of samsara—which is full of errors, delusions, and miseries—with one hand wipes the tears, and with the other, unshaken, shows the path of deliverance. On the one hand there is the conservative society, like a mass of inert matter; on the other, the restless, impatient, fire-darting reformer; the way to good lies between the two. I heard in Japan that it was the belief of the girls of that country that their dolls would be animated if they were loved with all their heart. The Japanese girl never breaks her doll. O you of great fortune! I too believe that India will awake again if anyone could love with all his heart the people of the country—bereft of the grace of affluence, of blasted fortune, their discretion totally lost, downtrodden, ever starved, quarrelsome, and envious. Then only will India awake, when hundreds of large-hearted men and women, giving up all desires of enjoying the luxuries of life, will long and exert themselves to their utmost for the well-being of the millions of their countrymen who are gradually sinking lower and lower in the vortex of destitution and ignorance. I have experienced even in my insignificant life that good motives, sincerity and infinite love can conquer the world. One single soul possessed of these virtues can destroy the dark designs of hypocrites and brutes.

—*Ibid.*, Vol. V, p. 127.

That education has an inherent relationship with the welfare of the society is not only based on theories but in practice also for anyone who believes in the philosophy of love as a compulsory component of altruism. Vivekananda adds something more for education that strives for a genuine involvement with the society. His concern is to uphold education as a means for coming closest to the society where our sincere dutifulness indicates our progress in education. The four necessary factors associated with the success of education as an instrument for social development are an endearing and sincere attitude to everyone in the society, a strong belief in the divine power inherent all the time in the every human being, which guides and accelerates love and service to the society, elimination of hatred, and control and calmness in involvement. Vivekananda characteristically upholds these factors as follows:

First, we have to bear in mind that we are all debtors to the world and the world does not owe us anything. It is a great privilege for all of us to be allowed to do anything for the world. In helping the world we really help ourselves. The second point is that there is a God in this universe. It is not true that this universe is drifting and stands in need of help from you and me. God is ever present therein, He is undying and eternally active and infinitely watchful. When the whole universe sleeps, He sleeps not; He is working incessantly; all the changes and manifestations are His. Thirdly, we ought not to hate anyone. This world will always continue to be a mixture of good and evil. Our duty is to sympathise with the weak and to love even the wrong-doer. The world is a grand moral gymnasium wherein we have all to take exercise so as to become stronger and stronger spiritually. Fourthly, we ought not to be fanatics of any kind, because fanaticism is opposed to love. You hear fanatics glibly saying, "I do not hate the sinner. I hate the sin," but I am prepared to go any distance to see the face of that man who can really make a distinction between the sin and the sinner. It is easy to say so. If we can distinguish well between quality and substance, we may become perfect men. It is not easy to do this. And further, the calmer we are and the less disturbed our selves, the more shall we love and the better will our work be.

—*Ibid.*, Vol. I, p. 80.

The concept of love through education for social synchronisation is entirely dependent on that of freedom. Unless the infinite spirit of every human being is taken into account in our education, love fails to manifest in our contemplation and action. That everyone is an embodiment of knowledge can hardly be reality without endearing knowledge in the hearth and warmth of love which serves as the centre of human enlightenment in extending every little "I" in the vast social milieu.

Admittedly, Vivekananda delvers a unique definition of love from the above-mentioned perspective:

All are our fellow passengers, our fellow travellers—all life, plants, animals; not only my brother man, but my brother brute, my brother plant; not only my brother the good, but my brother the evil, my brother the spiritual and my brother the wicked. They are all going to the same goal. All are in the same stream, each is hurrying towards that infinite freedom. We cannot stay the course, none can stay it, none can go back, however he may try; he will be driven forward, and in the end he will attain to freedom. Creation means the struggle to get back to freedom, the centre of our being, whence we have been thrown off, as it were. The very fact that we are here, shows that we are going towards the centre, and the manifestation of the attraction towards the centre is what we call love.

—*Ibid.*, p. 422.

The lesson of feeling for others as the education of service to the society is the education par excellence. Vivekananda strongly advocates the education of how to be a true social worker uninterruptedly and selflessly without being disappointed or elated by failure or success. As a matter of fact, his elucidation of a pursuer and devotee to work—a Karma-Yogi—upholds the lesson of non-attachment to one of his disciples:

When man has perforce to do some work, Karma-Yoga enjoins on him to do it in such a way as will bring freedom through the realisation of the Atman. As to your objection that none will be induced to work—the answer is, that whatever work you do has some motive behind it; but when by the long performance of work, one notices that one work merely leads to another, through a round of births and re-births, then the awakened discrimination of man naturally begins to question itself, "Where is the end to this interminable chain of work?" It is then that he appreciates the full import of the words of the Lord in the Gita: "Inscrutable is the course of work." Therefore when the aspirant finds that work with motive brings no happiness, then he renounces action. But man is so constituted that to him the performance of work is a necessity, so what work would he take up? He takes up some unselfish work, but gives up all desire for its fruits. For he has known then that in those fruits of work lie countless seeds of future births and deaths. Therefore the knower of Brahman renounces all actions. Although to outward appearances he engages himself in some work, he has no attachment to it. Such men have been described in the scripture as Karma-Yogins.

—*Ibid.*, Vol. VII, pp.179-180.

The education of service to the society, therefore, leads one to have a firm faith in being a selfless worker. In such a striving, the only lesson to be learnt is how to sacrifice whatever stands for personal interest and how to conquer over all constraints even by embracing death heroically. This is man-making education. This is education that fondles and respects we-feeling and we-loving. As Vivekananda poignantly asserts:

We must die, that is certain; let us die then for a good cause. Let all our actions—eating, drinking, and everything that we do—tend towards the sacrifice of our self. You nourish your own body by eating. What good is there in doing that if you do not hold it as a sacrifice to the well-being of others? You nourish your minds by reading books. There is no good in doing that unless you hold it also as a sacrifice to the whole world. For the whole world is one; you are rated a very significant part of it, and therefore it is right for you that you should serve your millions of brothers rather than aggrandise this little self.

You must not merely learn what the Rishis taught. Those Rishis are gone, and their opinions are also gone with them. You must be Rishis yourselves. You are also men as much as the greatest men that were ever born—even our Incarnations. What can mere book-learning do? What can meditation do even? What can the Mantras and Tantras do? You must stand on your own feet. You must have this new method—the method of man-making. The true man is he who is strong as strength itself and yet possesses a woman's heart. You must feel for the millions of beings around you, and yet you must be strong and inflexible and you must also possess obedience; though it may seem a little paradoxical—you must possess these apparently conflicting virtues.

—*Ibid.*, Vol. III, pp.446-448.

How to bring education to the hapless masses? How to enlighten those people in the society by means of education of warmth, sympathy and cooperation? Vivekananda reminds us of the winds of change in education brought forth by the modern age of mutual understanding and appreciation, where every society must be allowed to enjoy breadth of vision and fullness in education. In explaining the real role of education for social development, he significantly observes:

The education which does not help the common mass of people to equip themselves for the struggle for life, which does not bring the strength of character, a spirit of philanthropy, and the courage of a lion—is it worth the name? Real education is that which enables one to stand on one's own legs. The education that you are receiving now in schools and colleges is only making you a race of dyspeptics. You are working like machines merely, and living a jelly-fish existence.

The peasant, the shoemaker, the sweeper, and such other lower classes in India have much greater capacity for work and self-reliance than you. They have been silently working through long ages and producing the entire wealth of the land, without a word of complaint. Very soon they will get above you in position. Gradually capital is drifting into their hands, and they are not so much troubled with wants as you are. Modern education has changed your fashion, but new avenues of wealth lie yet undiscovered for want of the inventive genius. You have so long oppressed these forbearing masses; now is the time for their retribution. And you will become extinct in your vain search for employment, making it the be-all and end-all of your life.

—*Ibid.*, Vol. VII, pp. 147-148.

Unless the task of spreading education among the masses is taken in right earnest, the role of education for social synchronisation becomes an abject failure. What should be strategies for the education of the masses? What are the fundamental and vulnerable areas of interest in this regard? Vivekananda has a very distinct and positive suggestion for the education of the masses in the trans-national backdrop of education for social regeneration:

Engrossed in the struggle for existence, they [the masses] had not the opportunity for the awakening of knowledge. They have so long worked uniformly like machines guided by human intelligence, and the clever educated sections have taken the substantial part of the fruits of their labour. In every country this has been the case. But times have changed. The lower classes are gradually awakening to this fact and making a united front against this, determined to exact their legitimate dues. The masses of Europe and America have been the first to awaken and have already begun the fight. Signs of this awakening have shown themselves in India, too, as is evident from the number of strikes among the lower classes nowadays. The upper classes will no longer be able to repress the lower, try they ever so much. The well-being of the higher classes now lies in helping the lower to get to their legitimate rights.

Therefore I say, set yourselves to the task of spreading education among the masses. Tell them and make them understand, "You are our brothers—a part and parcel of our bodies, and we love you and never hate you." If they receive this sympathy from you, their enthusiasm for work will be increased a hundredfold. Kindle their knowledge with the help of modern science. Teach them history, geography, science, literature, and along with these the profound truths of religion. In exchange for that teaching, the poverty of the teachers will also disappear. By mutual exchange both parties will become friendly to each other.

—*Ibid.*, pp.148-149.

Do we devoutly follow and appropriately adhere to the guidelines of Vivekananda?

4

Education and Humanism: Vivekananda's Pointers

Education is inseparably associated with man. Bereft of education is dissociation with the essential components of how to be justified to humanism. Man cannot live alone. Education is the way to find out and determine the exact way of extinction of loneliness. Therefore, it is the only definite means of reducing oneself to a cipher so that loneliness becomes insignificant and is turned into a citadel of altruism, when every 'I' is merged in the well-being of all 'We'. That is humanism in the wee hours of efflorescence.

As a matchless connoisseur of humanism, Vivekananda draws our attention towards education of the right mind and that of the right kind. When he speaks of education as 'the manifestation of perfection already in man', he points out how education is closely related to humanism in the fullness and perfection of man. In this regard, he brings education and, for that end-in-view, the religion of humanism into the forethoughts of human ascent and excellence. The prayer with which we would be deeply associated is to have the strength for cultivating and disseminating the education of sympathy for those who have somehow or other been deprived of or denied education. As he poignantly proclaims:

> Let us pray, "Lead, Kindly Light"—a beam will come through the dark, and a hand will be stretched forth to lead us. I always pray for you: you must pray for me. Let each of us pray day and night for the down-trodden millions of India who are held fast by poverty, priestcraft and tyranny—pray day and night for them. I care more to preach religion to them than to the high and the rich. I am no metaphysician, no philosopher, nay, no saint. But I am poor, I love the poor. I see what they call the poor of the country, and how many there are who feel for them! What an immense difference in India! Who feels there for the two hundred millions of men and women sunken for ever in poverty and ignorance? What is the way out? Who feels for them? They cannot find light or education. Who will bring the light to them—who will travel from door to door bringing education to them? Let these people be your God—think for them, work for them, pray for them incessantly—the Lord will show you the way.
>
> —Swami Vivekananda: *The Complete Works of Swami Vivekananda*, Advaita Ashrama, Calcutta, Mayavati Memorial Edition, 1989, Vol V, pp. 57-58.

The education of selflessness that builds the strong foundation of humanism is the essence of Vivekananda's educational philosophy of human development. The spirit of self-sacrifice serves as the guiding spirit of human excellence. The secret of all good education lies in it. As Vivekananda characteristically elucidates in detail:

Ask nothing; want nothing in return. Give what you have to give; it will come back to you—but do not think of that now, it will come back multiplied in thousand-fold—but the attention must not be on that. Yet have the power to give; give, and there it ends. Learn that the whole of life is giving, that nature will force you to give. So, give willingly. Sooner or later you will have to give up. You come into life to accumulate. With clenched hands, you want to take. But nature puts a hand on your throat and makes your hands open. Whether you will it or not, you have to give. The moment you say, "I will not", the blow comes; you are hurt. None is there but will be compelled, in the long run, to give up everything. And the more one struggles against this law, the miserable one feels. It is because we dare not give, because we are not resigned enough to accede to this grand demand of nature, that we are miserable. The forest is gone, but we get heat in return. The sun is taking up water from the ocean, to return it in showers. You are a machine for taking and giving: you take in order to give. Ask, therefore, nothing in return; but the more you give, the more will come to you. The quicker you can empty the air out of this room, the quicker it will be filled up by the external air; and if you close all the doors and every aperture, that which is within will remain, but that which is outside will never come in, and that which is within will stagnate, degenerate, and become poisoned. A river is continually emptying itself into the ocean and is continually filling up again. Bar not the exit into the ocean. The moment you do that, death seizes you.

—*Ibid.*, Vol. II, pp. 5-6.

Not to be superhuman but to exercise the super-divine strength inherent in everyone is one of the principal lessons on exercising the spirit of dynamic humanism. For this, the education of the spirit of self-control which is the armour against all failures will definitely teach the lesson of how to win over all constraints internal or external whatsoever for the cause of human welfare. As Vivekananda adroitly points out:

It is very difficult, but we can overcome the difficulty by constant practice. We must learn that nothing can happen to us, unless we make ourselves susceptible to it. I have just said, no disease can come to me until the body is ready; it does not depend alone on the germs, but upon a certain predisposition which is already in the body. We get only that for which we are fitted. Let us give up our pride and understand this, that never is misery undeserved. There has been a blow undeserved; there never has been an evil for which I did not pave the way with my own hands. We ought to know that. Analyse yourselves and you will find that every blow you have received came to you because you have prepared yourselves for it. You did half, and the external world did the other half: that is how the blow came. That will sober us down. At the same time from the very analysis will come a note of hope, and the note of hope is: "I have no control of the external world, but that which is me and nearer unto me, my own world, is in my control. If the two together are required to make a failure, if the two together are necessary to give me a blow, I will not continue the one which is in my keeping; and how then can the blow come? If I get real control of myself, the blow will never come."

—*Ibid.*, pp. 7-8.

For an assured entry into the world of humanism, Vivekananda draws our attention towards exercise of the education of feeling. This enables us to shed all differences and work for the cause of the well-being of others. This also prepares us to forget our own petty interests and come straight towards amelioration of the sorrows and sufferings of the downtrodden humanity. In spelling out the three essential things for humane achievements, he first mentions the education of feeling and strongly asserts:

First, feel from the heart. What is in the intellect or reason? It goes a few steps and there it stops. But through the heart comes inspiration. Love opens the most impossible gates. Feel, therefore, my would-be patriots. Do you feel? Do you feel that millions and millions of the descendents of gods and of sages have become next-door neighbours to brutes? Do you feel that millions are starving to-day, and millions have been starving for ages? Do you feel that ignorance has come over the land as a dark cloud? Does it make you restless? Does it make you sleepless? Has it gone into your blood, course through your veins, becoming consonant with your heart-beats? Has it made you almost mad? Are you seized with the one idea of the misery of ruin, and have you forgotten all about your name, your fame, your wives, your children, your property, even your own bodies? Have you done that? That is the first step.

—*Ibid*, pp. 225-226.

Vivekananda also unfolds the spirit of humanism which is beyond the domain of intelligence and opens a new horizon of the mystic ascent of man by means of the awakening of Purusha. It is Strength Indomitable that paves path to the worship the Impersonal God—the highest prize of the education of humanism. In his exquisite elucidation of soham—I am He—he stirringly observes:

Strength, strength it is that we want so much in this life, for what we call sin and sorrow have one cause, and that is our weakness. With weakness comes ignorance and with ignorance comes misery. It will make us strong. Then miseries will be laughed at, then the violence of the will be smiled at, and the ferocious tiger will reveal, behind its tiger's nature, my own self. That will be the result. The soul that is strong has become one with the Lord; none else is strong. In your own Bible, what do you think was the cause of that strength of Jesus of Nazareth, that immense, infinite strength which laughed at traitors, and blessed those that were willing to murder him? It was that, "I am my Father and one"; it was that prayer, "Father, just I am one with you, so make them all one with me". That is the worship of the Impersonal God. Be one with the universe, be one with Him. And this Impersonal God requires no demonstrations, no proofs. He is nearer to us than even our senses, nearer to us than our own thoughts; it is in and through Him that we see and think. To see anything, I must first see Him. To see this wall, I first see Him, and then the wall, for He is the eternal subject. Who is seeing whom? He is here in the heart of our hearts. Bodies and minds change; miseries, happiness, good and evil come and go; days and years roll on; life comes and goes; but He does not. The same voice, "I am, I am", is eternal, unchangeable. In Him and through Him we see everything. In Him and through Him we sense, we think, we live, and we are. And that "I", which we mistake to be a little "I", limited, is not only my "I", but yours, the "I" of every one, of the animals, of the angels of the lowest, of the lowliest of the low. That "I am" is the same in the murderer as in the saint, the same in the rich as in the poor, the same in man as in woman, the same in man as in animals. From the lowliest amoeba to the highest angel, He resides in every soul, and eternally declares, "I am He". When we have understood that voice eternally present there, when we have learnt this lesson, the whole universe will have expressed its secret.

—*Ibid*, Vol. I, pp. 381-382.

Vivekananda's vision of humanism is always poignant with the philosophy of the divinity of man who is never alienated from reality as a divine source of perfection and purity of human life to be lived from now towards eternity. Love towards humans is thus turned towards the great "I", the "I" that teaches the lesson of the wonderful unison between the Lover and the Beloved. The eternal enquiry of the human mind on the exact identity of man in terms of human emotions and sensibilities finds a new but eternally true concept of humanism in the lesson of love. As Vivekananda explicitly unfolds:

When one loves the Lord, the whole universe becomes dear to one, because it is all His. "Everything is His, and He is my Lover; I love Him", says the Bhakta. In this way everything becomes sacred to the Bhakta, because all things are His. How, then, may we hurt anyone? How, then, may we not love another? With the love of God will come, as its effect, the love of everyone in the long run. The nearer we approach God, the more do we begin to see that all things abide in Him, our heart will become a perennial fountain of love. Man is transformed in the presence of this Light of Love and realises at last the beautiful and inspiring truth that Love, Lover and the Beloved are really one.

—*Ibid*, Vol. VIII, p.258.

Vivekananda teaches us a new philosophy of humanism that unveils the great truth that good and evil are both the creation of God. With such a creation, human life and death are evaluated quite significantly in association with human behaviour. The good part of life also introduces the other side—the side of evil—that allows the humane elements to be tested in terms of sorrows and sufferings which are nothing but the other sides of the experiences of life to share and experience in full freedom and conviction derived from erudition and edification. Vivekananda remarkably elucidates the concept of humanism in terms of good and evil as follows:

There are good and evil in this world. Sometimes evil becomes good, true; but other times good becomes evil also. All our senses produce evil sometime or other. Let a man drink wine. It is not bad [at first], but let him go on drinking, [and] it will produce evil....A man is born of rich parents; good enough. He becomes a fool, never exercises his body or brain. That is good producing evil. Think of this love of life; we go away and jump about and live a few moments; we work hard. We are born babies, entirely incapable. It takes us years to understand things again. At sixty or seventy we open our eyes; and then come the words, "Get out!" And there you are.

Now, who is responsible for all this good and evil, if God is ever the good? The Christians and the Mohammedans say there is a gentleman called Satan. How can you say there are two gentlemen working?

There must be one....The fire that burns the child also cooks the meal. How can you call the fire good or bad, and how can you say it was created by two different persons? Who creates all [so-called] evil? God. There is no other way out. He sends death and life, plague and epidemics, and everything. If such is God, He is the good; He is the evil; He is the beautiful; He is the terrible; He is life; and He is death.

—*Ibid.*, Vol. VI, p.54.

To consider oneself responsible for the evils of the world is to be on the right track of education for acceleration of humanism. Vivekananda reminds us of self-abnegation from this specific point of education for humanism. Education as he upholds always aims at the religion of sympathy that stands as a guiding principle of dynamic humanism. This is why Vivekananda inspires us to pursue the lesson of altruism as an antidote to self-assertion. In his own crystallised viewpoints:

One cannot divide the rights of the universe. To talk of "right" implies limitation. It is not "right" but "responsibility". Each is responsible for the evil anywhere in the world. No one can separate himself from his brother. All that unites with the universal is virtue; all that separates is sin. You are a part of the Infinite. This is your nature. Hence you are your brother's keeper.

The first end of life is knowledge; the second end of life is happiness. Knowledge and happiness lead to freedom. But not one can attain liberty until every being (ant or dog) has liberty. No one can be happy until all are happy. When you hurt anyone you hurt yourself, for you and your brother are one. He is indeed a Yogi who sees himself in the whole universe and the whole universe in himself. Self-sacrifice, not self-assertion, is the law of the highest universe. The world is so evil because Jesus' teaching, "Resist not evil", has never been tried. Selflessness alone will solve the problem. Religion comes with intense self-sacrifice. Desire nothing for yourself. Do all for others. This is to live and move and have your being in God.

—*Ibid.*, p. 83.

The education for appropriate living, moving and having one's being in God is an altogether new philosophy of humanism with which Vivekananda wants to make us acquainted. He also inspires us to learn the lesson of how to honour and develop our will force which leads to education of the right mind. To strengthen the will is to strengthen character. For this, our endeavour should be directed towards the learning of ourselves through all trials and constraints until we are hallowed with the effulgence of truth. That is what Vivekananda identifies as evolution in the education of humanism. In his own words:

We commit mistakes because we are weak, and we are weak because we are ignorant. Who makes us ignorant? We ourselves. We put our hands over our eyes and weep that it is dark. Take the hands away and there is light. The light exists always for us, the self-effulgent nature of the human soul. Do you hear what modern scientific men say? What is the cause of evolution? Desire. The animal wants to do something but does not find the environment favourable, and therefore develops a new body. Who develops it? The animal itself: its will. Continue to exercise your will and it will take you higher. The will is almighty. If it is almighty, you may say: why cannot I do everything? But you are thinking only of your little self. Look back on yourself from the state of the amoeba to the human being; who made all that? Your own will. Can you deny that it is almighty? That which has made you come up so high, can make you go higher still. What you want is character, strengthening of the will.

—*Ibid.*, Vol. II, pp. 356-357.

That everyone should contribute to the cause of humanity is the essence of humanism. Vivekananda makes us alert of the role of human welfare from this specific point. He also inspires us to form a new race of humankind with this enlivening spirit of humanism. And, for that end in view, our endeavour in education should be education of the right mind that cares for the advancement of humanism with an open-minded vision. As he adroitly remarks:

There is a common platform, a common ground of understanding, a common humanity, which must be the basis of our work. We ought to find out that complete and perfect human nature which is working only in parts here and there. It has not been given to one man to have everything in perfection. You have a part to play; I, in my humble way, another; here is one who plays a little part; there, another. The perfection is the combination of all these parts. Just as with individuals, so with races. Each race has a part to play; each race has one side of human nature to develop. And we have to take all these together; and, possibly in the distant future, some race will arise in which all these marvellous individual race perfections, attained by the different races, will come together and form a new race, the like of which the world has not yet dreamed. Beyond saying that, I have no criticism to offer about anybody. I have not travelled a little in my life; I have kept my eyes open; and the more I go about the more my mouth is closed.

—*Ibid.*, Vol. VIII, pp. 56-57.

The quest for the truth that there is divinity in every human being is one of the greatest adventures in education. For such an adventure, the role of education in warding off every type of superstition is undeniably very important. It advances humanism towards honouring the spiritual entity in everyone irrespective of any apparent difference whatsoever and howsoever. Once the dawn of spirituality so effulged in the education of humanism is endeared and ensured, the divinity awaiting grace and splendour in the bright noon of human ascent and excellence no longer eludes human endeavour. Vivekananda's educational philosophy points this great truth of humanism adorned and emboldened with a personal anecdote:

The more I live, the more I become convinced everyday that every human being is divine. In no man or woman, however vile, does that divinity die. Only he or she does not know how to reach it and is waiting for the Truth. And wicked people are trying to deceive him or her with all sorts of fooleries. If one man cheats another for money, you say he is a fool and a blackguard. How much greater is the inequity of one who wants to fool others spiritually! This is too bad. It is the one test, that truth must make you strong and put you above superstition. The duty of the philosopher is to raise you above superstitions; what infinite souls you are! And to be tricked by twinkling stars! It is a shameful condition. You are divinities; the twinkling stars owe their existence in you.

I was once travelling in the Himalayas, and the long road stretched before us. We poor monks cannot get any one to carry us, so we had to make all the way on foot. There was an old man with us. The way goes up and down hundreds of miles, and when that old monk saw what was before him, he said, "Oh, sir, how to cross it; I cannot walk any more; my chest will break." I said to him, "Look down at your feet." He did so, and I said, "The road that is under your feet is the road that you have passed over and is the same road that you see before you; it will soon be under your feet." The highest things are under your feet, because you are Divine Stars; all these things are under your feet.

You can swallow the stars by the handful if you want; such is your real nature. Be strong, get beyond all superstitions, and be free.

—*Ibid.*, pp. 186-187.

That man progresses from truth to truth and never from error to truth is the radical lesson of humanism as Vivekananda upholds in his philosophy of education. This is a new religion of humanism which heightens the role of every human being. What Vivekananda wants from a learner is to have the unending spirit of enquiry that shows the avenue of entering deep into the heartland of humanity. In his own endeavour, he has proved that all contradictions that one encounters in course of pursuit of different religious ideas are actually not contradictions but supplementary to arriving at a greater and ultimately a universal concept of the conjoint spirit of humanism awaiting continual crystallisation. As he characteristically asserts:

Every religion has a soul behind it, and that soul may differ from the soul of another religion; but are they contradictory? Do they contradict or supplement each other?—that is the question. I look up the question when I was quite a boy, and have been studying all my life. Thinking that my conclusion may be of some help to you, I place it before you. I believe that they are not contradictory; they are supplementary. Each religion, as it were, takes up one part of the great universal truth, and spends its whole force in embodying and typifying that part of the great truth. It is, therefore, addition not exclusion. That is the idea. System after system arises, each embodying a great idea, and ideals must be added to ideals. And this is the march of humanity. Man never progresses from error to truth but from truth to truth, from lesser truth to higher truth—but never from error to truth.

—*Ibid.*, Vol. II, p. 365.

The education of the great Vedanta philosophy of humanism that Vivekananda emphasises in his thoughts and experiments on "Thou art That"—Tat Tvam Asi—is the surest means of understanding and appreciating the consciousness of the Infinite in every human being. The lesson of oneness with the universe alone can teach everyone of the real worth of man. Unless this oneness is exercised in earnestness and open-mindedness, the spirit of humanism makes no sense in human life. In elucidating this philosophy of the Vedanta as the exponent of living humanism, Vivekananda strongly asserts:

The Vedanta claims that there has not been one religious inspiration, one manifestation of the divine man, however great, but it has been the expression of that infinite human nature; and all that we call ethics and morality and doing good to others is also but the manifestation of this oneness. There are moments when every man feels that he is one with the universe, and he rushes forth to express it, whether he knows it or not. This expression of oneness is what we call love and sympathy, and it is the basis of all our ethics and morality. This is summed up in the Vedanta philosophy by the celebrated aphorism, Tat Tvam Asi, "Thou art That".

To every man, this is taught: Thou art one with this Universal Being, and, as such, every soul that exists is your soul; and every body that exists is your body; and in hurting anyone, you hurt yourself, in loving anyone, you love yourself. As soon as a current of hatred is thrown outside, whomsoever else it hurts, it also hurts yourself; and if love comes out from you, it is bound to come back to you. For I am the universe; this universe is my body, I am the Infinite, only I am not conscious of it now; but I am struggling to get this consciousness of the Infinite, and perfection will be reached when full consciousness of this Infinite comes.

—*Ibid.*, Vol. I, pp. 389-390.

To quicken our growth as human beings, education has a great role to play. It must be living and dynamic, responsive and responsible to the ascent and excellence of man in every direction of fullness and perfection. Vivekananda disseminates this inherent and most living spirit of education for humanism by tracing the history of the growth and development of man right from childhood:

Each man in his childhood runs through the stages through which his race has come up; only the race took thousands of years to do it, while the child takes a few years. The child is first the old savage man—and he crushes a butterfly under his feet. The child is at first like the primitive ancestors of his race. As he grows, he passes through different stages until he reaches the development of his race. Only he does it swiftly and quickly. Now, take the whole of humanity as a race, or take the whole of the animal creation, man and the lower animals, as one whole. There is an end towards which the whole is moving. Let us call it perfection. Some men and women are born who anticipate the whole progress of mankind. Instead of waiting and being born over and over again for ages until the whole human race has attained to that perfection, they, as it were, rush through them in a few short years of their life. And we know that we can hasten these processes, if we be true to ourselves. If a number of men, without any culture, be left to live upon an island, and are given barely enough food, clothing and shelter, they will gradually go on and on, evolving higher and higher stages of civilisation. We know also, that this growth can be hastened by additional means. We help the growth of trees, do we not? Left to nature, they would have grown, only they would have taken a longer time; we help them to grow in a shorter time than they would otherwise have taken. We are doing all the time the same thing, hastening the growth of things by artificial means. Why cannot we hasten the growth of man? We can do that as a race. Why are teachers sent to other countries? Because by these means we can hasten the growth of races. Now, can we not hasten the growth of individuals? We can. Can we put a limit to the hastening? We cannot say how much a man can grow in one life. You have no reason to say that this much a man can do and no more. Circumstances can hasten him wonderfully. Can there be any limit then, till you come to perfection? So, what comes of it? That a perfect man, that is to say, the type that is to come of this race, perhaps millions of years hence, that man, can come today.

—*Ibid.*, Vol. II, pp. 18-19.

For a higher vision of life as humanism really stands for, education must be closely related and responsive to the study of the mind. The study, again, should guarantee the essence of humanism which is perfection of the whole man and not a fragmentary end-in-view of accomplishment. Therefore, the experience of pleasure should embrace that of pain, happiness do that of sufferings, and, the lesson that is learnt best in course of such an experience is one of enlightened humanism. Vivekananda unfolds this education of humanism very remarkably by means of identifying the spiritual efflorescence inherent in every human being:

Good and evil have an equal share in moulding character and in some cases misery is a greater teacher than happiness. In studying the great characters the world has produced, I dare say, in the vast majority of cases, it would be found that it was misery that taught more than happiness, it was poverty that taught more than wealth, and it was blows that brought out their inner fire more than praise.

—*Ibid.*, Vol. I, p. 27.

Elsewhere, Vivekananda speaks of 'the light within', the light which is the gift of the 'spiritual tempest' bringing about the realisation of the All Serene by means of the education of the Omnipresent and Omniscient:

When there comes affliction in the heart, when the storm of sorrow blows all around, and it seems light will be seen no more, when hope and courage are almost gone, it is then, in the midst of this great spiritual tempest, that the light of Brahman within gleams. Brought up in the lap of luxury, lying on a bed of roses and never shedding a tear, who has ever become great, who has ever unfolded the Brahman within? Why do you fear to weep? Weep! Weeping clears the eyes and brings about intuition. Then the vision of diversity—man, animal, tree—slowly melting away, makes room for the infinite realisation of Brahman everywhere and in everything. Then—

Samang pasyat hi sarvatra samavasthitamisvaram

Na hinastyatmanatmanang tato yati parang gatim.

——"Verily, seeing the same God equally existent everywhere, he does not injure the Self by the self, and so goes to the Supreme Goal" (Gita, XIII. 28)

—*Ibid.*, Vol. IV, p. 492.

For a sincere and practical realisation of religion, Vivekananda directs education as a direct involvement of life in all its manifestations. In such an involvement, purity in thought and action is the process of acquisition of and experiments in knowledge, where there is no compromise with the lower instincts of human behaviour. Perseverance is the key factor for such an action that ensures humanism well protected and advanced in education of quality and excellence. Vivekananda explains this point very succinctly:

> The conditions necessary for the taught are purity, a real thirst after knowledge, and perseverance. No impure soul can be really religious. Purity in thought, speech, and act is absolutely necessary for any one to be religious. As to the thirst after knowledge, it is an old law that we all get whatever we want. None of us can get anything other than what we fix our hearts upon. To pant for religion truly is really a very difficult thing, not at all so easy as we generally imagine. Hearing religious talks or reading religious books is no proof yet of a real want felt in the heart; there must be a continuous struggle, a constant fight, an unremitting grappling with our lower nature, till the higher want is actually felt and the victory is achieved. It is not a question of one or two days, of years, or of lives; the struggle may have to go on for hundreds of life-times. The success sometimes may come immediately, but we must be ready to wait patiently even for what may look like an infinite length of time. The student who sets out with such a spirit of perseverance will surely find success and realisation at last.
>
> —*Ibid.*, Vol. III, p. 48.

To rise up to the occasion of teaching humanism as above, the teacher must be sinless. His purity is greatly necessary for the learners as a genuine model of motivation. His spirituality as a crystallised process of exercise of humanism serves best as an inspiring spurt for every learner. Vivekananda categorically remarks in this connection as follows:

The question is often asked, "Why should we look into the character and personality of a teacher? We have only to judge of what he says, and take that up." This is not right. If a man wants to teach me something of dynamics, or chemistry, or any other physical science, he may be anything he likes, because what the physical sciences require is merely an intellectual equipment; but in the spiritual sciences it is impossible from first to last that there can be any spiritual light in the soul that is impure. What religion can an impure man teach? The sine qua non of acquiring spiritual truth for one's self or for imparting it to others is the purity of heart and soul. A vision of God or a glimpse of the beyond never comes until the soul is pure. Hence with the teacher of religion we must first see what he is, and then what he says. He must be perfectly pure, and then alone comes the value of his words, because he is only then the true "transmitter". What can he transmit if he has not spiritual power in himself? There must be the worthy vibration of spirituality in the mind of the teacher, so that it may be sympathetically conveyed to the mind of the taught. The function of the teacher is indeed an affair of the transference of something, and not one of mere stimulation of the existing intellectual or other faculties in the taught. Something real and appreciable as an influence comes from the teacher and goes to the taught. Therefore the teacher must be pure.

—*Ibid.*, pp. 50-51.

The education of the heart which is the education of true humanism is the forte of Vivekananda's philosophy of education. Indeed, it is this education which contributes a great deal to the education of love. Mere intellectual education may produce scholars of high eminence but that education must make ample room for, and, of course, guarantee purity bereft of which all scholarship fails to illuminate the self. Therefore, he judiciously prescribes for preference of the education of the heart to that of the brain in the event of a conflict between the two:

When there is conflict between the heart and the brain, let the heart be followed, because intellect has only one state, reason, and within that, intellect works, and cannot get beyond. It is the heart which takes one to the highest plane, which intellect can never reach; it goes beyond intellect, and reaches to what is called inspiration. Intellect can never become inspired; only the heart when it is enlightened, becomes inspired. An intellectual, heartless man never becomes an inspired man. It is always the heart that speaks in the man of love; it discovers a greater instrument than intellect can give you, the instrument of inspiration.

Just as intellect is the instrument of knowledge, so is the heart the instrument of inspiration. In a lower state it is a much weaker instrument than intellect. An ignorant man knows nothing, but he is a little emotional by nature. Compare him with a great professor—what wonderful power the latter possesses! But the professor is bound by his intellect, and he can be a devil and an intellectual man at the same time; but the man of heart can never be a devil; no man with emotion was ever a devil. Properly cultivated, the heart can be changed, and will go beyond intellect; it will be changed into inspiration. Man will have to go beyond intellect in the end. The knowledge of man, his powers of perception, of reasoning and intellect and heart, all are busy churning the milk of the world. Out of long churning comes butter, and this butter is God. Men of heart get the "butter", and the "buttermilk" is left for the intellectual.

—*Ibid.*, Vol. I, pp. 412-413.

What type of a teacher does Vivekananda conform to his philosophy of humanism? How can education be the life blood, as it were, of every human thought and experience? For a thrilling and emulating response to these and allied queries on the real role of education for human excellence, Vivekananda submits his own account of how he is blessed with a teacher par excellence for all time and all generation to come in the history of humankind:

The teacher is not a man who comes just to teach me, and I pay him so much, and there it ends. In India, it is really like an adoption. The teacher is more than my own father, and I am truly his child, his son in every respect. I owe him obedience and reverence first, before my own father even; because, they say, the father gave me this body, but he showed me the way to salvation, he is greater than father. And we carry this love, this respect for our teacher all our lives. And that is the only organisation that exists. I adopt my disciples. Sometimes the teacher will be a young man and the disciple a very old man. But never mind, he is the son, and he calls me "Father", and I have to address him as my son, my daughter, and so on.

Now, I happened to get an old man to teach me, and he was very peculiar. He did not go much for intellectual scholarship, scarcely studied books; but when he was a boy he was seized with the tremendous idea of getting truth direct. First he tried by studying his own religion. Then he got the idea that he must get the truth of other religions; and with that idea he joined all the sects, one after another. For the time being he did exactly what they told him to do—lived with the devotees of these different sects in turn, until interpenetrated with the particular ideal of that sect. After a few years he would go to another sect. When he had gone through with all that, he came to the conclusion that they were all good. He had no criticism to offer to any one; they are all so many paths leading to the same goal. And then he said, "That is a glorious thing, that there should be so many paths, because if there were only one path, perhaps it would suit only an individual man. The more the number of paths, the more the chance for every one of us to know the truth. If I cannot be taught in one language, I will try another, and so on."

—*Ibid.*, Vol. VIII, pp. 78-79.

What, then, is the fundamental end-in-view of education for efflorescence of humanism? What should prompt one to be a true humanist as the prized outcome of education as it is always desirable? Vivekananda has a very categorical and positive answer. It is to appositely rise up to the occasion of realisation of the three essentials in oneself—Existence Absolute, Knowledge Absolute and Bliss Absolute. These essentials of education would contribute to humane sensibilities in abundance throughout life and beyond life. This would also prompt one to respect and restore the divinity in oneself in all confidence and conviction. As Vivekananda adroitly asserts:

Do not pity anyone. Look upon all as your equal, cleanse yourself of the primal sin of inequality. We are all equal and must not think, "I am good and you are bad, and I am trying to reclaim you". Equality is the sign of the free. Jesus came to publicans and sinners and lived with them. He never set himself on a pedestal. Only sinners see sin. See not man, see only the Lord. We manufacture our own heaven and can make a heaven even in hell. Sinners are only to be found in hell, and as long as we see them around us, we are there ourselves. Spirit is not in time, nor in space. Realise "I am Existence Absolute, Knowledge Absolute, Bliss Absolute—I am He, I am He". Be glad at birth, be glad at death, rejoice always in the love of God. Get rid of the bondage of body; we have become slaves to it and learnt to hug our chains and love our slavery; so much so that we long to perpetuate it, and go on with "body" "body" for ever. Do not cling to the idea of "body", do not look for a future existence in any way like this one; do not love or want the body, even of those dear to us. This life is our teacher, and dying only makes room to begin over again. Body is our schoolmaster, but to commit suicide is folly, it is only killing the "Schoolmaster". Another will take his place. So until we have learnt to transcend the body, we must have it, and losing one, will get another. Still we must not identify ourselves with the body, but look upon it only as an instrument to be used in reaching perfection.

—*Ibid.*, pp. 18-19.

The education of work which Vivekananda introduces heralds a new horizon of humanism. Work for the sake of work alone teaches the lesson of how to reduce oneself to a cipher. The fountain of humanism, as it were, springs forth in selfless service. The major components of such selfless service are love and truth, benevolence and sympathy besides other ones that convey the spirit of education in self-control and self-sacrifice because the greatest power of education for humanism is the undying patience and look ahead without caring for the self. Vivekananda makes an exhaustive analysis on the education of work for the cause of humanity in his philosophy of man, and characteristically unfolds this as follows:

Work for work's sake. There are some who are really the salt of the earth in every country and who work for work's sake, and do not care for name, or fame, or even to go to heaven. They work just because good will come out of it. There are others who do good to the poor and help mankind from still higher motives, because they believe in doing good and love good. The motive for name and fame seldom brings immediate results, as a rule; they come to us when we are old and have almost done with life. If a man works without any selfish motive in view, does he not gain anything? Yes, he gains the highest. Unselfishness is more paying, only people have not the patience to practise it. It is more paying from the point of view of health also. Love, truth, and unselfishness are not merely moral figures of speech, but they form our highest ideal, because in them lies such a manifestation of power. In the first place, a man who can work for five days, or even for five minutes, without any selfish motive whatever, without thinking of future, of heaven, of punishment, or anything of the kind, has in him the capacity to become a powerful moral giant. It is hard to do it, but in the heart of our hearts we know its value, and the good it brings. It is the greatest manifestation of power—this tremendous restraint; self-restraint is a manifestation of greater power than all outgoing action. A carriage with four horses may rush down a hill unrestrained, or the coachman may curb the horses. Which is the greater manifestation of power, to let them go or to hold them? A cannon-ball flying through the air goes along distance and falls. Another is cut short in its flight by striking against a wall, and the impact generates intense heat. All outgoing energy following a selfish motive is frittered away; it will not cause power to return to you; but if restrained, it will result in development of power. This self-control will tend to produce a mighty will, a character which makes a Christ or a Buddha. Foolish men do not know this secret; they nevertheless want to rule mankind. Even a fool may rule the whole world if he works and waits. Let him wait a few years, restrain that foolish idea of governing; and when that idea is wholly gone, he will be a power in the world.

—*Ibid.*, Vol. I, pp. 32-33.

To be a real possessor of an astounding power in the world, mankind needs a new education spear-headed by Vivekananda to the advancement of humanism right now. Are we ready to respond and act accordingly?

5

Education and Religion: Vivekananda's Viewpoints

Education is an enquiry within—eternal and ceaseless, painstaking and persevering. To Swami Vivekananda, it is something more than that. It is to manifest in manifold dimensions the incomparable and unparalleled power within. It is that power which can make all impossible possible, all failures definite pointers of success. He also upholds the personality in every human being and, for this, the service to mankind in all purity and sincerity is the service to the All Serene.

Admittedly, Vivekananda eyes education as an inseparable exponent of religion. Such education is always pregnant with the vibrant appeal of religion that caters to all the greatest virtues and poignant prayers of man: work is worship. When he speaks on the ideal of education and explains the role of great teachers of religion, the synchronised philosophy of education and religion becomes all the more explicit and transparent:

The ideal of all education, all training should be man-making. But, instead of that, we are always trying to polish up the outside. What use in polishing up the outside when there is no inside? The end and aim of all training is to make the man grow. The man who influences, who throws the magic, as it were, upon his fellow-beings, is a dynamo of power, and when that man is ready, he can do anything and everything he likes; that personality put upon anything will make it work.

Now, we see that though this is a fact, no physical laws that we know of will explain this. How can we explain it by chemical and physical knowledge? How much of oxygen, hydrogen, carbon, how many molecules in different positions, and how many cells, etc., etc. can explain this mysterious personality? And we still see, it is a fact, and not only that, it is the real man; and it is that man that lives and moves and works, it is that man that influences, moves his fellow-beings, and passes out, and his intellect and books and works are but traces left behind. Think of this. Compare the great teachers of religion with the great philosophers. The philosophers scarcely influenced anybody's inner man, and yet they wrote marvellous books. The religious teachers, on the other hand, moved countries in their lifetime. The difference was made by personality. In the philosopher it is a faint personality that influences; in the great prophets it is tremendous.

In the former we touch the intellect, in the latter we touch life. In the one case, it is simply a chemical process, putting certain chemical ingredients together which may gradually combine and under proper circumstances bring out a flash of light or may fail. In the other, it is like a torch that goes round quickly, lighting others.

—Swami Vivekananda: *The Complete Works of Swami Vivekananda*, Advaita Ashrama, Calcutta, Mayavati Memorial Edition, 1989, Vol. II, pp15-16.

That education has an abiding influence as an exponent of religion of the highest order is the essential point of significance of Vivekananda's philosophy of education. This ennobles and heightens the role of religion not as an arduous exercise of what is written in books on religion but exercising, orienting and crystallising it in terms of individuality. Therefore, the individual is the architect of what religion truly stands for and represents the best of humankind free from all antagonisms and misgivings cradled in coarseness and devaluation of personality. The struggle to be individuals of the right kind and of the right mind is the core of religion par excellence, and, for that end-in-view, learning should never stand in the way of efflorescence of one's individuality. Vivekananda has always advocated on discipline of the mind in order to be good individuals, and not to be mere learners by sacrificing our indomitable power of thinking individually. Only then we will be in a position to crystallise ourselves through education of the self by the self. As he characteristically warns and advises in course of a lecture delivered in San Francisco area on April 10, 1900:

> Mind you, there is no value in learning. You are all mistaken in learning. The only value of knowledge is in the strengthening, the disciplining, of the mind. By all this eternal swallowing it is a wonder that we are not all dyspeptics. Let us stop, and burn all the books, and get hold of ourselves and think. You all talk [about] and get distracted over losing your "individuality". You are losing it every moment of your lives by this eternal swallowing. If any one of you believes what I teach, I will be sorry. I will only be too glad if I can excite in you the power of thinking for yourselves....My ambition is to talk to men and women, not to sheep. By men and women, I mean individuals. You are not little babies to drag all the filthy rags from the street and bind them up into a doll!
>
> The whole point is to discipline the mind. That truth which you swallow from others will not be yours. You cannot teach truth from my mouth; neither can you learn truth from my mouth. None can teach another. You have to realise truth and work it out for yourself according to your own nature.....All must struggle to be individuals—strong, standing on your own feet, thinking your own thoughts, realising your own Self. No use swallowing doctrines others pass on—standing up together like soldiers in jail, sitting down together, all eating the same food, all nodding their heads at the same time. Variation is the sign of life. Sameness is the sign of death.

Once I was in an Indian city, and an old man came to me. He said, "Swami, teach me the way." I saw that that man was as dead as this table before me. Mentally and spiritually he was really dead. I said, "Will you do what I ask you to do? Can you steal? Can you drink wine? Can you eat meat?"

The man [exclaimed], "What are you teaching?"

I said to him, "Did this wall ever steal? Did the wall ever drink wine?"

"No, sir."

Man steals, and he drinks wine, and becomes God. "I know you are not the wall, my friend. Do something!" I saw that if that man stole, his soul would be on the way to salvation.

How do I know that you are individuals—all the same thing, all standing up and sitting down together? That is the road to death! Do something for your souls! Do wrong if you please, but do something! You will understand me by and by, if you do not just now. Old age has come upon the soul, as it were. It has become rusty. The rust must be [rubbed off], and then we go on.

—*Ibid.*, Vol. VI, pp. 64-66.

The vibrant spirit of education which Vivekananda unfolds, serves the manifestation of individuality without being distorted by rituals, dogmas, rules and regulations that have nothing to do directly with efflorescence of education and individuality. When religion stands for that education which upholds realisation, the purpose and significance of both education and religion are best negotiated for effulgence of individuality. The true exercise for assent or dissent is the essential component of how to realise the All Serene residing within everyone of us. Vivekananda adroitly spells out this symphony of education and religion:

Reason, theories, documents, doctrines, books, religious ceremonies, are all helps to religion: religion itself consists in realisation. We all say, "There is a God." Have you seen God? That is the question. You hear a man say, "There is God in heaven." You ask him if he has seen Him, and if he says he has, you would laugh at him and say he is a maniac. With most people religion is a sort of intellectual assent and goes no further than a document. I would not call it religion. Religion does not depend on our intellectual assent or dissent. You say there is a soul. Have you seen the soul? How is it we all have souls and do not see them? You have to answer the question and find out the way to see the soul. If not, it is useless to talk of religion. If any religion is true, it must be able to show us the soul and show us God and the truth in ourselves. If you and I fight for all eternity about one of these doctrines and documents, we shall never come to any conclusion. People have been fighting for ages, and what is the outcome? Intellect cannot reach there at all. We have to go beyond the intellect; the proof religion is in direct perception. The proof of the existence of this wall is that we see it; if you sat down and argued about its existence or non-existence for ages, you could never come to any conclusion; but directly you see it, it is enough. If all the men in the world told you it did not exist, you would not believe them, because you know that the evidence of your own eyes is superior to all the doctrines and documents in the world.

—*Ibid.*, Vol. IV, p. 34.

The infinite presence of perception in oneself is realisation which stands the desirable outcome of education. Here learning becomes irrelevant and useless in the sense that inner perception has nothing to do with it. But that it is an education of all educations and paves path to religion of the highest and most serene order is what Vivekananda earnestly elucidates:

Learning has no place in religion; for the majority learning is a block in the way.....A man may have read all the libraries in the world and may not be religious at all, and another, who cannot perhaps write his own name, senses religion and realises it. The whole of religion is our own inner perception. When I use the words "man-making religion", I do not mean books, nor dogmas, nor theories. I mean the man who has realised, has fully perceived, something of that infinite presence in his own heart.

The man at whose feet I sat all my life—and it is only a few ideas of his that try to teach—could [hardly] write his name at all. All my life I have not seen another man like that, and I have travelled all over the world. When I think of that man, I feel like a fool, because I want to read books and he never did. He never wanted to lick the plates after other people had eaten. That is why he was his own book. All my life I am repeating what Jack said and John said, and never say anything myself. What glory is it that you know what John said twenty-five years ago and what Jack said five years ago? Tell me what you have to say.

—*Ibid.*, Vol. VI, p. 64.

Like a dedicated and steadfast follower of education that actually stands for the religion of man, Vivekananda unfolds one of the most important components of education and, therefore, of religion. It is love. The lesson of love is actually the lesson of religion par excellence. It is this lesson which shows the avenues and ascent of man the divine being within that awaits efflorescence with all perfume of perfection and brilliance. As he elucidates in one of his most remarkable poems, "To a Friend":

Listen, friend, I will speak my heart to thee,

I have found in my life this truth supreme—

Buffeted by waves, in this whirl of life,

There's one ferry that takes across the sea.

Formulas of worship, control of breath,

Science, philosophy, systems valid,

Relinquishment, possession, and the like,

All these are but delusions of the mind—

Love, Love—that's the one thing, the sole treasure.

In Jiva and Brahman, in man and God,

In ghosts, and wraiths, and spirits, and so forth,

In Devas, beasts, birds, insects, and in worms,

This Prema dwells in the heart of them all.

Say, who else is the highest God of gods?

Say, who else moves all the universe?

The mother dies for her young, robber robs—

Both are but the impulse of the same Love!

—*Ibid.*, Vol. IV, pp. 494-95.

Ignorance to be replaced by knowledge, as true education signifies, is the religion of the highest order. Such religion is self-realisation which is the most prized entity of man. Vivekananda emphasises on this religion of the self, the realisation of the Atman, which genuinely represents divinity inherent in the pursuit of knowledge. All purposes of knowledge become less significant than knowledge that teaches and prepares us how to be true and justified to the Atman. Then, and then only, education for knowledge pure and serene becomes a higher essence of reality. As he categorically asserts;

Ignorance constitutes the only darkness, which covers all things and makes them look mysterious. When everything is lighted by Knowledge, the sense of mystery vanishes from the face of things. Even such an inscrutable thing as Maya, which brings the most impossible things to pass, disappears. Know Him, think of Him, by knowing whom everything else is known. And when that Atman is realised, the purport of all scriptures will be perceived as clearly as a fruit on the palm of one's hand. The Rishis of old attained realisation, and must we fail? We are also men. What has happened once in the life of one individual must, through proper endeavour, be realised in the life of others. History repeats itself. This Atman is the same in all, there is only a difference of manifestation in different individuals. Try to manifest this Atman, and you will see your intellect penetrating into all subjects. The intellect of one who has not realised the Atman is one-sided, whereas the genius of the knower of Atman is all-embracing. With the manifestation of the Atman you will find that science, philosophy, and everything will be easily mastered. Proclaim the glory of the Atman with the roar of a lion, and impart fearlessness unto all beings by saying, "Arise, awake, and stop not till the goal is reached".

—*Ibid.*, Vol. VII. P.138.

Elsewhere, Vivekananda exposes the reality of knowledge in terms of ascent beyond the realm of relative knowledge with which we are generally satisfied as the ultimate nature of education:

All our world comes from truth and untruth coupled together. Samsara (life) is the result of the contradictory forces acting upon us, like the diagonal motion of a ball in a parallelogram of forces. The world is God and is real, but that is not the world we see; just as we see silver in the mother-of-pearl where it is not. This is what is known as Adhyasa or superimposition, that is, a relative existence dependent upon a real one, as when we recall a scene we have seen; for the time it exists for us, but that existence is not real. Or some say, it is as when we imagine heat in water, which does not belong to it; so really it is something which has been put where it does not belong, "taking the thing for what it is not". We see reality, but distorted by the medium through which we see it.

You can never know yourself except as objectified. When we mistake one thing for another, we always take the thing before us as the real, never the unseen; thus we mistake the object for the subject. The Atman never becomes the object. Mind is the internal sense, the outer senses are its instruments. In the subject is a trifle of the objectifying power that enables him to know "I am"; but the subject is the object of its own Self, never of the mind or the senses. You can, however, superimpose one idea on another idea, as when we say, "The sky is blue", the sky itself being only an idea. Science and nescience there are, but the Self is never affected by any nescience. Relative knowledge is good, because it leads to absolute knowledge; but neither the knowledge of the senses nor of the mind, nor even of the Vedas is true, since they are all within the realm of relative knowledge. First get rid of the delusion, "I am the body", then only can we want real knowledge. Man's knowledge is only a higher degree of brute knowledge.

—*Ibid.*, pp. 32-33.

As a pioneer in education for self-realisation, Vivekananda also clarifies the role of knowledge as a means of removing the darkness of ignorance among the lowly and the ignorant, the poor and the disadvantaged. At the same time, he inspires us to be an untiring learner of practical religion which opens the new world of self-realisation and we can in all sincerity understand the true meaning and concept of freedom. As a radical educationist, he unfolds the ascent of man who has within himself the Kingdom of Heaven in terms of self-realisation as an infinite spirit that never admits any defeat. As he vibrantly asserts:

You must see God. The spirit must be realised, and that is practical religion. It is not what Christ preached that you call practical religion: "Blessed are the poor in spirit for theirs is the Kingdom of Heaven." Was it a joke? What is the practical religion you are thinking of? Lord, help us! "Blessed are the poor in heart, for they shall see God." That means street-cleaning, hospital building, and all that? Good works, when you do them with a pure mind. Don't give the man twenty dollars and buy all the papers in San Francisco to see your name! Don't you read in your own books how no man will help you? Serve as worship of the Lord Himself in the poor, the miserable, the weak. That done, the result is secondary. That sort of work done without any thought of gain, benefits the soul. And even of such is the Kingdom of Heaven.

The Kingdom of Heaven is within us. He is there. He is the soul of all souls. See Him in your own soul. That is practical religion. That is freedom. Let us ask each other how much we are advanced in that; how much we are worshippers of the body, or real believers in God, the spirit; how much we believe ourselves to be spirit. That is selfless. That is freedom. That is real worship. Realise yourself. That is all there is to do. Know your self as you are—infinite spirit. This is practical religion. Everything else is impractical, for everything else will vanish. That alone will never vanish. It is eternal.

—*Ibid.*, Vol. IV, p. 246.

The education of understanding and appreciating the existence of the Kingdom of Heaven within us that Vivekananda inspires us to follow with all earnestness and devotion is one of the greatest components of all religions. In fact, all religions teach the great lesson of preparing oneself for exercising the practical aspects like freedom and selflessness which cannot be undertaken unless there is a strong belief in the existence of the Kingdom of Heaven within every one of us. As religion is the innermost essence of education, the devotion to worship the great saints for their invaluable guidelines to the path of perfection in religion actually leads to success in the education of the self by having the education of the soul. Such an education makes us alert and devoted to learning the lessons of self-strength, resourcefulness, courage, conviction, service to humanity and, above all, indifference to everything except the All Serene. Vivekananda's own words clarify this point characteristically:

> The true eternal principles have to be held before the people. First of all we have to introduce the worship of the great saints. Those great-souled ones who have realised the eternal truths are to be presented before the people as the ideals to be followed—Sri Ramachandra, Sri Krishna, Mahavira, Sri Ramakrishna and others. Keep aside for the present the Vrindavan aspect of Sri Krishna and spread far and wide the worship of Sri Krishna roaring out the Gita with the voice of a lion, and bring into daily use the worship of Shakti—the Divine Mother, the source of all power. We now mostly need the ideal of the hero with the tremendous spirit of Rajas thrilling through his veins from head to foot—the hero who will dare and die to know the truth, the hero whose armour is renunciation, whose sword is wisdom.
>
> —*Ibid.*, Vol. V, p. 388.

The new religion in which Vivekananda is interested is neither following the religious scriptures nor believing in God, but learning the truth that there is infinite strength in oneself. This is one of the most important lessons that enlivens and heightens the glory of man as the best creation of God. Moreover, this brings forth and sustains faith in oneself and serves as the potent force of ascent and excellence for which true religion always stand. Self-love is love divine and such consciousness is the religion that teaches one how to be loved and living to others. This is, indeed, the education of religion to which one should all the time be devoted. Vivekananda elucidates very succinctly:

> The old religions said that he was an atheist who did not believe in God. The new religion says that he is the atheist who does not believe in himself. But it is not selfish faith. It means faith in all because you are all. Love for yourself means love for all, love for animals, love for everything, for you are all one. It is the great faith which will make the world better. The ideal of faith in ourselves is of the greatest help to us. If faith in ourselves had been more extensively taught and practised, I am sure a very large portion of the evils and miseries that we have would have vanished. Throughout the history of mankind if any motive power has been more potent than another in the lives of great men and women, it is that faith in themselves. Born with the consciousness that they were to be great, they became great.
>
> —*Ibid.*, Vol. II, p. 301.

To strengthen the brain is to strengthen religion. The education of religion, as Vivekananda advocates, always inspires us to be physically strong in order to be mentally alert and agile, active and vigorous. In fact, all education depends on cultivation of the religion of strength and not that of weakness in which religion itself becomes a symbol of weakness.

Therefore, action is more important than contemplation, involvement in doing more urgent than in whiling away the precious time in and for worship. As Vivekananda categorically asserts:

> We speak of many things parrot-like but never do them. Speaking and not doing has become a habit with us. What is the cause? Physical weakness. This sort of weak brain is not able to do anything. We must strengthen it. First of all our young men must be strong. my advice to you. You will be nearer to Heaven through football than through the study of the Gita. You will understand Gita better with your biceps, your muscles a little stronger. You will understand the mighty genius and the mighty strength of Krishna better with a little strong blood in you. You will understand the Upanishads better and the glory of the Atman, when your body stands firm on your feet and you feel yourselves as men.
>
> —*Ibid.*, Vol. III, p. 343

Not to be emotional but to be down-to-earth and realistic is the essence of education and religion. Vivekananda inspires us to be religious with that education which teaches us to be practical in religion of regeneration of the self and the country as well by eliminating the darkness of religion that drives one to exercise emotional behaviour and endearing tireless strivings for strength of mind for service towards mankind. That is religion. That is education in perfect symphony with education of the mind as well as of the heart. Vivekananda categorically directs us to exercise that lesson for cultivation of true religion:

> Playing on the khol and kartal and dancing in the frenzy of the kirtana has degenerated the whole people. In trying to imitate the highest sadhana, the preliminary qualification for which is absolute purity, they have been swallowed in dire tamas. Are not drums made in the country? Are not trumpets and kettle-drums available in India? Make the boys hear the deep-toned sound of these instruments. Hearing from boyhood the sound of effeminate forms of music, the country is well-nigh converted into a country of women. The Damaru and horn have to be sounded, drums are to be beaten 'so as to raise the deep and martial notes, and with 'Mahavira', Mahavira' on our lips and shouting 'Hara, Hara, Vyom, Vyom', the quarters are to be reverberated. The music which awakens only the softer feelings of man is to be stopped now for sometime. The people are to be accustomed to hear the Dhrupad music.
>
> —*Ibid.*, Vol. VII, p. 232-233.

Admittedly, the lesson of strength is one of the greatest and most fruitful lessons that one can learn religion. It is the only effective antidote to fear and doubt, weakness and indecision. Vivekananda himself has learnt that lesson of fearlessness and strength of mind from the Upanishads. It is the lesson that never allows one to dwarf the indomitable spirit and struggle for proclaiming the eternal victory of man the Divine. As Vivekananda frankly exposes:

Strength, strength is what the Upanishads speak to me from every page. It is the only literature in the world, where you find the word 'Abhih', 'Fearless', used again and again. In no other scripture in the world is this adjective applied either to God or man. And in my mind rises from the past the vision of the great emperor of the West, Alexander the Great, and I see as it were in a picture the great monarch standing on the banks of the Indus, talking to one of our sannyasins in the forest: the old man he was talking to, perhaps naked, sitting upon a block of stone, and the Emperor astonished at his wisdom tempting him with gold and honour, to come over to Greece. And this man smiles at his gold and smiles at his temptations, and refuses. And then the Emperor standing in his authority as Emperor says, 'I will kill you if you do not come', and the man bursts into a laugh and says, 'You never told such a falsehood in your life as you tell just now. Who can kill me? For I am spirit unborn and undecaying.' That is strength.

—*Ibid.*, Vol. III, pp. 237-238.

The strength that we receive from the education of religion is what promises the poignancy of the truth that all education rightly directed towards understanding and appreciating the reflection of the mind must be justified to the education of the heart. Therefore, mere cultivation of intellect without caring for nursing the education of the heart which is the true religion of education would simply be meaningless. It will never be endearing and vibrant. It will not respond the goodness of all, which is the fundamental end-in-view of every religion and education. A harmonised endeavour in education for cultivation of the heart and intellect as Vivekananda suggests is not only desirable but also obligatory for man-making living education:

> We may be most intellectual people the world ever saw and yet we may not come to God at all. On the other hand, irreligious men have been produced from the most intellectual training. It is one of the evils of Western civilisation—intellectual education alone without taking care of the heart. It only makes men ten times more selfish. When there is conflict between the heart and the brain, let the heart be followed. It is the heart that takes one to the highest plane, which intellect can never reach. It goes beyond the intellect and reaches what is called inspiration.
>
> —*Ibid.*, Vol. I, p. 412.

The relation between education and religion, according to Vivekananda, is one of continual and challenging crystallisation of the self in terms of both in isolation and unison as well. With education of acceptance of all religions as the guiding spirit of perfection of life for all time anywhere and everywhere, religion becomes the eternal fountain of human ascent and excellence. Such education shows the way to spiritual progress of humans in acceptance of the essence of every religion with reverence and sincere devotion, practice and dissemination in the process of the making of man in tune with the great exponents and teachings of religion. In this regard Vivekananda's thrilling words are very significant:

I accept all religions that were in the past and worship them all. I worship God with every one of them, in whatever form they worship Him. I shall go to the mosque of the Mohammedan; I shall enter the Christian's church and kneel before the crucifix. I shall enter the Buddhist temple, where I shall take refuge in Buddha and his Law. I shall go into the forest and sit down in meditation with the Hindu, who is trying to see the Light which enlightens the heart of everyone.

Not only shall I do all these but I shall keep my heart open for all that may come in the future. Is God's book finished? Or is it still a continuous revelation going on? It is a marvellous book—these spiritual revelations of the world. The Bible, the Vedas, the Koran and all other sacred books are but so many pages, and an infinite number of pages remain yet to be unfolded. Let us take in all that has been in the past, enjoy the light of the present and open every window of the heart for all that will come in the future. Salutations to all the prophets of the past, to all the great ones of the present and to all that are to come in the future.

—*Ibid.*, Vol. II, pp. 373-374.

Vivekananda reminds us of the real role of intellect in education which more often than not pays more attention to and interest in matter and science and technology than in exploring the mind for the learning and experiencing the minds and the hearts of others within oneself. That is religion crystallised and instilled in oneself for the cause of humanity; it not merely teaches us to be conscious of oneself but to be devoted to the study of the superconscious bereft of which the living presence of God within oneself always remains beyond experience and erudition.

That the culture of intellect in and through education should go beyond the range of matter or for that purpose satisfaction of learning for artificialities is the newer avenue of making a significant quest for religion for which education is yet to play its important role. Vivekananda, therefore, inspires us to be more interested in the cultivation of the heart than in that of matter. Otherwise, the truth of life to be lived as it ought to be lived remains far beyond our reach. As he remarkably elucidates:

If you are not pure, and you know all the sciences in the world, that will not help you at all; you may be buried in all the books you read, but that will not be of much use. It is the heart that reaches the goal. Follow the heart. A pure heart sees beyond the intellect; it gets inspired; it knows things that reasons can never know, and whenever there is conflict between the pure heart and the intellect, always side with the pure heart, even if you think what your heart is doing is unreasonable. When it is desirous of doing good to others, your brain may tell you that it is not politic to do so, but follow your heart, and you will find that you make less mistakes than by following your intellect. The pure heart is the best mirror for the reflection of truth, so all these disciplines are for the purification of the heart. And as soon as it is pure, all truths flash upon it in a minute; all truth in the universe will manifest in your heart, if you are sufficiently pure.

The great truths about atoms, and the finer elements, and the fine perceptions of men, were discovered ages ago by men who never saw a telescope, or a microscope, or a laboratory. How did they know all these things? It was through the heart; they purified the heart. It is open to us to do the same today; it is the culture of the heart, and not that of the intellect that will lessen the misery of the heart.

—*Ibid.*, Vol. I, p. 414.

Education should be geared towards that direction whereby the true concept of the latter becomes evident and free from doubts and myths it is yet to unfold and exercise religion as a science of all sciences as it teaches us the lesson of how to go beyond consciousness.

Again, the spirit of super-consciousness that we can learn and exercise through the education of religion allows us to enter into a new world of knowledge and experience by means of which we go beyond the world of consciousness and religion then does not remain rigid and static but living and dynamic. That education of religion will enable us to understand and appreciate the great truth that true religion is always transcendental and evolutionary. This education brings forth a new religion of knowing and disseminating the eternal spirit of God within everyone of us. In the words of Vivekananda:

The field of religion is beyond our senses, beyond even our consciousness. We cannot sense God. Nobody has seen God with his eyes or ever will see; nobody has God in his consciousness. I am not conscious of God, nor you, nor anybody. Where is God? Where is the field of religion? It is beyond the senses, beyond consciousness. Consciousness is only one of the many planes in which we work; you will have to transcend the field of consciousness, to go beyond the senses, approach nearer and nearer to your own centre, and as you do that, you will approach nearer and nearer to God. What is the proof of God? Direct perception, Pratyaksha. The proof of this wall is that I perceive it. God has been perceived that way by thousands before, and will be perceived by all who want to perceive Him. But this perception is no sense-perception at all; it is super-sensuous, super-conscious, and all this training is needed to take us beyond the senses. By means of all sorts of past work and bondages we are being dragged downwards; these perceptions will make us pure and light. Bondages will fall off by themselves, and we shall be buoyed up beyond this plane of super-perception to which we are tied down, and then we shall see, and hear, and feel things which men in the three ordinary states (viz. waking, dream and sleep) neither feel, nor see, nor hear. Then we shall speak a strange language, as it were, and the world will not understand us, because it does not know anything but the senses. True religion is entirely transcendental. Every being that is in the universe has the potentiality of transcending the senses; even the little worm will one day transcend the senses and reach God. No life will be a failure; there is no such thing as failure in the universe. A hundred times man will hurt himself, a thousand times he will tumble, but in the end he will realise that he is God.

—*Ibid.*, pp.415-416.

To realise the All Serene within oneself is definitely the invaluable lesson of the education of religion. It is that education which teaches us how to renounce everything in order to attain spirituality. Vivekananda terms this education as one of self-sacrifice for purity and perfection. As he characteristically advises us:

Give up, renounce the world. Now we are like dogs strayed into a kitchen and eating a piece of meat, looking round in fear lest at any moment some one may come and drive them out. Instead of that, be a king and know you own the world. This never comes until you give it up and it ceases to bind. Give up mentally, if you do not physically. Give up from the heart of your hearts. Have Vairagya (renunciation). This is the real sacrifice, and without it, it is impossible to attain spirituality. Do not desire, for what you desire you get, and with it comes terrible bondage. It is nothing but bringing "noses on us", as in the case of the man who had three boons to ask. We never get freedom until we are self-contained. "Self is the Saviour of self, none else."

Learn to feel yourself in other bodies, to know that we are all one. Throw all other nonsense to the winds. Spit out your actions, good or bad, and never think of them again. What is done is done. Throw off superstition. Have no weakness even in the face of death. Do not repent, do not brood over past deeds, and do not remember your good deeds; be azad (free). The weak, the fearful, the ignorant will never reach Atman. You cannot undo, the effect must come, face it, but be careful never to do the same thing again. Give up the burden of all deeds to the Lord; give all, both good and bad. Do not keep the good and give only the bad. God helps those who do not help themselves.

—*Ibid.*, Vol. VII, pp.90-91.

That our real knowledge is perception which actually stands for religion is the essence of both religion and education as they are one and the same. The real learner and practitioner of religion never learns from others save from himself. He always learns by himself and within himself. Therefore, what is necessary for a learner in quest of true religion is to explore himself untiringly and, for this, he must develop the power of his mind through concentration and adherence to reason. The other allied lessons are devotion and love besides control of the body and finally realisation of religion culminating in the world of illumination leading to spirituality. As Vivekananda exquisitely elucidates in detail:

Perception is our only real knowledge or religion. Talking about it for ages will never make us know our soul. There is no difference between theories and atheism. In fact, the atheist is the truer man. Every step I take in the light is mine for ever. When you go to a country and see it, then it is yours. We have each to see for ourselves; teachers can only "bring the food", we must eat it to be nourished. Argument can never prove God save as a logical conclusion.

It is impossible to find God outside of ourselves. Our own souls contribute to all the divinity that is outside of us. We are the greatest temple. The objectification is only a faint imitation of what we see within ourselves.

Concentration of the powers of the mind is our only instrument to help us to see God. If you know one soul (your own), you know all souls, past, present, and to come. The will concentrates the mind, certain things excite and control this will, such as reason, love, devotion, breathing. The concentrated mind is a lamp that shows us every corner of the soul.

Stick to your reason until you reach something higher; and you will know it to be higher, because it will not jar with reason. The stage beyond consciousness is inspiration (Samadhi); but never mistake hysterical trances for the real thing. It is a terrible thing to claim this inspiration falsely, to mistake instinct for inspiration. There is no external test for inspiration, we know it ourselves; our guardian against mistake is negative—the voice of reason. All religion is going beyond reason, but reason is the only guide to get there. Instinct is like ice, reason is the water, and inspiration is the subtlest form or vapour; one follows the other. Everywhere is this eternal sequence—unconsciousness, consciousness, intelligence—

matter, body, mind—and to us it seems as if the chain began with the particular link we first lay hold of. Arguments on both sides are of equal weight, and both are true. We must reach beyond both, to where there is neither the one nor the other. These successions are all Maya.

Religion is above reason, supernatural. Faith is not belief, it is the grasp of the Ultimate, an illumination. First hear, then reason and find out all that reason can give about the Atman; let the flood of reason flow over It, then take what remains. If nothing remains, thank God you have escaped a superstition. When you have determined that nothing can take away the Atman, that It stands every test, hold fast to this and teach it to all. Truth cannot be partial; it is for the good of all. Finally, in perfect rest and peace meditate upon It, concentrate your mind upon It, make yourself one with It. Then no speech is needed; silence will carry the truth. Do not spend your energy in talking, but meditate in silence. And do not let the rush of the outside world disturb you. When your mind is in the highest state, you are unconscious of it. Accumulate power in silence and become a dynamo of spirituality.

—*Ibid.*, pp. 59-61.

The quest for spirituality in course of the education of religion both as being and becoming transfused and transcended is the hallmark of Vivekananda's philosophy of education. He delves deep into the role of Nature in terms of the mind and vice versa in order to arrive at the great truth that knowledge is not merely a stepping stone of being and becoming but a revelation of consciousness that is controlled and bound by our senses. Therein lies the limitations of knowledge. For its superiority and crystallisation it must pave path to the beyond. That exercise ceaseless and ardent would transcend knowledge beyond senses and senses beyond consciousness towards attainment of spirituality which is the prized outcome of religion. Vivekananda unfolds this truth as follows:

Nature outside cannot give us any answer as to the existence of the soul, the existence of God, the eternal life, the goal of man, and all that. This mind is continually changing, always in a state of flux; it is finite, it is broken into pieces. How can nature tell of the Infinite, the Unchangeable, the Unbroken, the Indivisible, the Eternal? It never can. And whenever mankind has striven to get an answer from the dull dead matter, history shows how disastrous the results have been. How comes, then, the knowledge which the Vedas declare? It comes through being a Rishi. This knowledge is not in the senses; but are the senses the be-all and the end-all of the human being? Who dare say that the senses are the all-in-all of man? Even in our lives, in the life of every one of us here, there come moments of calmness, perhaps, when we see before us the death of one we loved, when some shock comes to us, or when extreme blessedness comes to us. Many other occasions there are when the mind, as it were, becomes calm, feels for the moment its real nature; and a glimpse of the Infinite beyond, where words cannot reach nor the mind go, is revealed to us. This happens in ordinary life, but it has to be heightened, practised, perfected. Men found out ages ago that the soul is not bound or limited by the senses, no, not even by consciousness. We have to understand that this consciousness is only the name of one link in the infinite chain. Being is not identical with consciousness, but consciousness is only one part of Being. Beyond consciousness is where the bold search lies. Consciousness is bound by the senses. Beyond that, beyond the senses, men must go in order to arrive at truths of the spiritual world, and there are even now persons who succeed in going beyond the bounds of the senses. These are called Rishis, because they come face to face with spiritual truths.

—*Ibid.*, Vol. III, pp. 252-253.

A radical and iconoclast in education and religion, Vivekananda inspires us to give all our hearts to the learning of love rather than undergoing intellectual exercise apart from the end-in-view of human welfare. He also advises us to have belief in ourselves which is religion itself to be strong enough to work with steadfast and ceaseless devotion for the cause of the well-being of others. That education is yet to be introduced. That education alone will bring about a new concept of religion whereby we can deepen our power of thought for ascent and excellence of inwardness. In this regard, Vivekananda's vibrant words have an eternal force:

Society must be outgrown. We must crush law and become outlaws. We allow nature, only in order to conquer her. Renunciation means that none can serve both God and Mammon.

Deepen your power of thought and love. Bring your own lotus to blossom: the bees will come of themselves. Believe first in yourself, then in God. A handful of strong men will move the world. We need a heart to feel, a brain to conceive, and a strong arm-to do the work. Buddha gave himself for the animals. Make yourself a fit agent to work. But it is God who works, not you. One man contains the whole universe. One particle of matter has all the energy of the universe at its back. In a conflict between the heart and the brain follow your heart.

Yesterday, competition was the law. Today, cooperation is the law. Tomorrow, there is no law. Let sages praise thee, or let the world blame. Let fortune itself come, or let poverty and rags stare thee in the face. Eat the herbs of the forest, one day, for food; and the next, share a banquet for fifty courses. Looking neither to right hand nor to the left, follow thou on!

—*Ibid.*, Vol. VIII, pp. 223-224.

How to be a sincere learner of religion? How to succeed in learning religion? Vivekananda's advice in this connection is very significant:

The conditions necessary in the taught are purity, a real thirst after knowledge, and perseverance. No impure soul can be religious; that is the one great condition; purity in every way is absolutely necessary. The other condition is a real thirst after knowledge.

Who wants? That is the question. We get whatever we want—that is an old, old law. He who wants, gets. To want religion is a very difficult thing, not so easy as we generally think. Then we always forget that religion does not consist in hearing talks, or in reading books, but it is a continuous struggle, a grappling with our own nature, a continual fight till the victory is achieved. It is not a question of one or two days, of years, or of lives, but it may be hundreds of lifetimes, and we must be ready for that. It may come immediately, or it may not come in hundreds of lifetimes; and we must be ready for that. The student who sets out with such a spirit finds success.

—*Ibid*., Vol. IV, p. 24.

That religion is realisation is to be learnt from the assimilation of the fact that the worship of God is to visualize Him in and through man. This is also true in case of knowledge that shows the avenue of realisation of God in man, where excess of intellectual jugglery leads to religious abstraction. At the same time man loses his identity with God. Vivekananda goes a step further in unfolding the two extremes of religion and education. His observation is very explicit and significant:

Two classes of men do not worship God as man—the human brute who has no religion, and the Paramahamsa (highest Yogi) who has gone beyond humanity, who has thrown off his mind and body and gone beyond the limits of nature. All nature has become his Self. He has neither mind nor body, and can worship God as God, as can a Jesus or a Buddha. They did not worship God as man. The other extreme is the human brute. You know how the extremes look alike. Similar is the case with the extreme of ignorance and the other extreme of knowledge; neither of these worships anybody. The extremely ignorant do not worship God, not being developed enough to feel the need for so doing. Those that have attained the highest knowledge also do not worship God—having realised and become one with God. God never worships God. Between these two poles of existence, if anyone tells you he is not going to worship God as man, take care of him. He is an irresponsible talker, he is mistaken; his religion is for frothy thinkers, it is intellectual nonsense.

—*Ibid.*, pp. 30-31.

Education and religion are so inter-related that a harmonious blending of the two ensures both. In fact, the education of religion and the religion of education are indivisible and together they contribute to the wholeness of one's being. It is also the signal to how to go beyond one's being for spiritual attainment. When Vivekananda reminds us of Thou art That—Om Tat Sat—the highest end-in-view of both education and religion is justified. As he solemnly muses:

Few only know the truth. The rest will hate

And laugh at thee, great one; but pay no heed.

Go thou, the free, from place to place, and help

Them out of darkness, Maya's veil. Without
The fear of pain or search for pleasure, go
Beyond them both, Sannyasin bold ! Say—
"Om Tat Sat, Om!"
Thus, day by day, till Karma's power spent
Release the soul for ever. No more is birth,
Nor I, nor thou, nor God, nor man. The "I"
Has All become, the All is "I" and Bliss.
Know thou art That, Sannyasin bold! Say—
"Om Tat Sat, Om!"

—*Ibid*., "The Song of the Sannyasin", p. 395.

For the adventure to be made in the religion of education, religion is to be explored by everyone every time anywhere and everywhere. There is no room for doubt or hesitation. The only endeavour would be to forge ahead with sincerity and devotion. Religion, then, would be as explicit as one's simple way of living and striving for the Great I within and everywhere. Vivekananda makes a clarion call for this Great I born of what he terms as chittasuddhi. That will enable us to learn about the true identity of God in man. In his own words:

Let all our vain gods disappear for the time from our minds. This is the only god that is awake, our own race—"everywhere his hands, everywhere his feet, everywhere his ears, he covers everything." All other gods are sleeping. What vain gods shall we go after and yet cannot worship the god that we see all round us, the Virat? When we have worshipped this, we shall be able to worship all other gods. Before we can crawl half a mile, we want to cross the ocean like Hanuman! It cannot be. Everyone going to be a Yogi, everyone going to meditate! It cannot be. The whole day mixing with the world with Karma Kanda, and in the evening sitting down and blowing through your nose! Is it so easy? Should Rishis come flying through the air, because you have blown three times through the nose? Is it a joke? It is all nonsense. What is needed is Chittasuddhi, purification of the heart. And how does that come? The first of all worship is the worship of the Virat—of those all around us. Worship It. Worship is the exact equivalent of the Sanskrit word, and no other English word will do. These are all our gods—men and animals; and the first gods we have to worship are our countrymen. These we have to worship, instead of being jealous of each other and fighting each other. It is the most terrible Karma for which we are suffering, and yet it does not open our eyes!

—*Ibid.*, Vol. III, pp. 300-301.

When would we be enlightened with the true vision of education and religion as Vivekananda in his clarion call beckons us?

6

Vibrant Education: Vivekananda's Quest

Education is a matter of enquiry–intrinsic and extrinsic, sincere and serene, devoted and dedicated. It allows one to explore oneself from different perspectives. It inspires one to delve deep into the world of knowledge and wisdom, information and experience, analysis and synthesis. It also encourages one to be particular about how one should be justified to oneself in order to be justified to others from the same dimensions, if not otherwise, and vice-versa.

To Swami Vivekananda, education is an unending, untiring and thrilling adventure. It is more than mere theories and information. It is practical and vibrant, dynamic and altruistic. As a matter of fact, he advocates education as a sound vehicle of making an adventure into the world of light. Only then it can be an exponent of humanism. He characteristically disseminates his invaluable observation on this point very poignantly as follows:

Look upon every man, woman and everyone as God. You cannot help anyone, you can only serve: serve the children of the Lord, serve the Lord Himself, if you have the privilege. If the Lord grants that you can help anyone of His children, blessed you are; do not think too much of yourselves. Blessed you are that privilege was given to you when others had it not. Do it only as worship. I should see God in the poor, and it is for my salvation that I go and worship them. The poor and the miserable are for our salvation, so that we may serve the Lord, coming in the shape of the diseased, coming in the shape of the lunatic, the leper and the sinner! Bold are my words; and let me repeat that it is the greatest privilege in our life that we are allowed to serve the Lord in all these shapes. Give up the idea by ruling over others you can do any good to them. But you can do just as much as you can in the case of the plant; you can supply the growing seed with the materials for the making up of its body, bringing to it the earth, the water, the air that it wants. It will take all that it wants by its own nature. It will assimilate and grow by its own nature.

Bring all light into the world. Light, bring light! Let light come into everyone; the task will not be finished till everyone has reached the Lord. Bring light to the poor; and bring more light to the rich, for they require it more than the poor. Bring light to the ignorant, and more light to the educated, for the varieties of the education of our time are tremendous! Thus bring light to all and leave the rest unto the

Lord, for in the words of the same Lord, "To work you have the right and not to the fruits thereof."

—Swami Vivekananda: *The Complete Works of Swami Vivekananda*, Mayavati Memorial Edition, Advaita Ashrama, Calcutta, 1989, Vol. VIII, p. 146.

Apart from the fact that Vivekananda closely encapsulates education for the welfare of humankind, his vision of education as the only means of bringing about vibrant changes in the society goes a long way in upholding the spirit of divinity of every human being in the society. Elucidating the end-in-view of education in terms of society, he emphasizes on action that cares for 'the feeling of unity':

It is the feeling of a unity towards which we are all going. Every action of our lives–the most material, the grossest as well as finest, the highest, the most spiritual is alike tending this one ideal, the finding of unity. A man is single. He marries. Apparently, it may be a selfish act, but at the same time the impulsion, the motive power, is to find that unity. He has children, he has friends, he loves his country, he loves his world, and ends by loving the whole universe. Irresistibly we are impelled towards that perfection which consists in finding the unity, killing this little and making ourselves broader and broader. This is the goal, the end towards which the universe is rushing. Every atom is trying to go and join itself to the next atom. Atoms after atoms combine, making huge balls, the earths, the suns, the moons, the stars, the planets. They, in their turn, are trying to rush towards each other, and, at last, we know that the whole universe, mental and material, will be found into one.

—*Ibid.*, Vol. VI, pp. 4-5.

The quest for that vibrant education which makes a union between the mental and material universe is what Vivekananda wants to uphold in his philosophy of education. For this quest, introspection is the first vital lesson that he encourages to pursue in right earnest. This will not only enable one to be justified to the universe but will also be in fusion with the sentient Being making all inroads to visualizing the One, the Ever Effulgent. As he significantly elucidates:

We must learn how to turn the eye to see inwards. The eagerness of the eyes to see outwards should be restricted. When you walk in a busy street, it is difficult to hear the man speak with whom you are walking, because of the passing carriages. He cannot hear you because there is so much noise. The mind is going outwards, and you cannot hear the man who is next to you. In the same way, this world around us is making such a noise that it draws the mind outwards. How can we see the Self? This going outwards must be stopped. That is what is meant by turning the eyes inwards, and then alone the glory of the Lord within will be seen....

There cannot be two beings which are infinite, and the result is, there is really only one Self, and you, I, and the universe are but one, appearing as many. "As the one fire entering into the world manifests itself in various ways, even so that one Self, the Self of all, manifests Itself in every form." But the question is: If this Self is perfect and pure, and the One Being of the universe, what becomes of It when It goes into the impure body, the wicked body, the good body, and so on? How can it remain perfect? "The one sun is the cause of vision in every eye, yet it is not touched by the defects in the eyes of any." If a man has prejudice he sees everything as yellow; the cause of his vision is the sun, but his seeing everything as yellow does not touch the sun. Even so the One Being, though the Self of everyone, is not touched by the purities or impurities outside. "In this world where everything is evanescent, he who knows Him who never changes, in this world of insentiency, he who knows the one insentient Being, in this world of many, he who knows this One and sees Him in his own soul unto him belongs eternal bliss, to none else, to none else. There the sun shines not, nor the stars, nor the lightning flashes what to speak of fire? He shining, everything shines; through His light everything becomes effulgent. When all the desires that trouble the heart cease, then the mortal becomes immortal, and here one attains Brahman. When all the crookedness of the heart disappears, when all knots are cut asunder, then alone the mortal becomes immortal. This is the way. May this study bless us, may it maintain us; may it give us strength, may it become energy to us; may we not hate each other; peace unto all.

—*Ibid.*, Vol. II, pp. 411-12.

The education for the good of one and all is Vivekananda's clarion call to every human being. That is the true religion. That alone ensures how to eliminate religiosity and superstition, ignorance and hatred. That is the way to emancipation from darkness to light, littleness to vastness, rudeness to humility.

The education of sacrifice coupled with that of character is the surest guideline to education par excellence. Such education, as Vivekananda advocates, makes us prepared for fullness of human life. In his own words expressed in a letter to Miss Noble on June 07, 1896:

My ideal indeed can be put into a few words and that is: to preach into mankind their divinity, and how to make it manifest in every movement of life.

This world is in chain of superstition. I pity the oppressed, whether man or woman, and I pity more the oppressors. One idea that I see clear as daylight is that misery is caused by ignorance and nothing else. Who will give the world light? Sacrifice in the past has been the Law, it will be, alas, for ages to come. The earth's bravest and best will have to sacrifice themselves for the good of many, for the welfare of all. Buddhas by the hundred are necessary with eternal love and pity.

Religions of the world have become lifeless mockeries. What the world wants is character. The world is in need of those whose life is one burning love, selfless. That love will make every word tell like thunderbolt.

It is no superstition with you, I am sure. You have the making in you of a world-mover, and others will also come. Bold words and bolder deeds are what we want. Awake, awake, great ones! The world is burning with misery. Can you sleep? Let us call and call till the sleeping gods awake, till the god within answers to the call. What more is in life? What greater work?

—*Ibid.*, Vol. VII, p. 501.

Education, to be meaningful, purposeful, effective, dynamic and vibrant as Vivekananda has all the time wanted everywhere, must be liberated from mechanical, dull and drab rote learning. As a matter of act, he has given topmost priority to innovation in teaching, where creativity and critical consciousness eliminate all possibilities of artificialities in learning. Freedom of thought and expression is the key to vibrant education. Lifeless education at any level—primary, secondary, vocational, higher or anything whatsoever—kills the very essence of potentiality and possibility of making an adventure into life and work, and allows cramming and crushing humane sensibilities. The religion of education is thus lost in artificialities and abstractions. Vivekananda, therefore, characteristically suggests:

We have to do only so much for the boys that they may learn to apply their own intellect to the proper use of their hands, legs, ears, eyes, etc., and finally everything will become easy. But the root is religion. Religion is as the rice, and everything else, like the curries. Taking only curries causes indigestion, and so is the case of taking rice alone. Our pedagogues are making parrots of our boys and ruining their brains by cramming a lot of subjects into them. Looking from one standpoint, you should rather be grateful to the Viceroy for his proposal of reforming the University system, which means practically abolishing higher education; the country will, at least, feel some relief by having breathing time. Goodness gracious! What a fuss and fury about graduating, and after a few days, all cools down! And after all that, what is it they learn but that what religion and customs we have are all bad, and what the Westerners have are all good! At last they cannot keep the wolf from the door! What does it matter if this higher education remains or goes? It would be better if the people got a little technical education, so that they might find work and earn their bread instead of dawdling about and crying for service.

—*Ibid.*, Vol. V, pp. 366-67.

Elsewhere, in a letter to Alisinga, Vivekananda poignantly remarks on vibrant education full of the promise of education of character and religion:

Let us pray, "Lead, Kindly Light"—a beam will come through the dark, and a hand will be stretched forth to lead us. I always pray for you; you must pray for me. Let each one of us pray day and night for the downtrodden millions in India who are held fast by poverty, priest-craft and tyranny—pray day and night for them. I care more to preach religion to them than to the high and the rich. I am no metaphysician, no philosopher, nay, no saint. But I am poor, I love the poor. I see what they call the poor of the country and how many there are who feel for them! What an immense difference in India! Who feels there for the two hundred millions of men and women sunken for ever in poverty and ignorance? Where is the way out? Who feels for them? They cannot find light or education. Who will bring the light to them—who will travel from door to door bringing education to them? Let these people be your God—think of them, work for them, pray for them incessantly–the Lord will show you the way. Him I call a Mahatman (great soul) whose heart bleeds for the poor, otherwise he is a Duratman (wicked soul). Let us unite our wills in continued prayer for their good. We may die unknown, unpitied, unbewailed, without accomplishing anything—but not one thought will be lost. It will take effect sooner or later. My heart is too full to express my feeling; you know it, you can imagine it. So long as the millions live in hunger and ignorance, I hold every man a traitor who, having been educated at their expense, pays not the least heed to them.

—*Ibid.*, p. 58

To explore 'the gymnasium of the world' as Vivekananda suggests as one of the fundamental ends-in-view of vibrant education is to serve the All Serene in the best possible way, and to serve so is to be genuinely devoted to the work. An attitude thus developed through devotion and dedication to work of the noblest kind would enable one to achieve perfect freedom, the goal of Karma-Yoga. The synchronization between the self and the soul by means of dedication and devotion to work for the cause of perfect freedom as Vivekananda advocates unfolds an incomparable chapter of vibrant education:

The highest men cannot work, for in them there is no attachment. Those whose whole soul is gone into the Self, those whose desires are confined in the Self, who have become ever associated with the Self, for them there is no work. Such are indeed the highest of mankind; but apart from them everyone else has to work. In so working we should never think that we can help on even the last thing in this universe. We cannot. We only help ourselves in this gymnasium of the world. This is the proper attitude of work. If we work in this way, if we always remember that our present opportunity to work thus is a privilege which has been given to us, we shall never be attached to anything. Millions like you and me think that we are great people in the world; but we all die and in five minutes the world forgets us. But the life of God is infinite. "Who can live a moment, breathe a moment, if this all powerful One does not will it?" He is the ever active Providence. All power is His and within His command. Through His command the windows blow, the sun shines, the earth lives, and death stalks upon the earth. He is the all in all; He is all and in all. We can only worship Him. Give up all fruits of work; do good for its own sake; then alone will come perfect non-attachment. The bonds of the heart will thus break, and we will reap perfect freedom.

—*Ibid.*, Vol. I, pp. 106-07.

The quest for freedom by means of vibrant education that cares for humble submission of the self to the Supreme Self is certainly very difficult and endless but it alone is the perfect avenue of fusion with the All Seer. It will prepare the learner to appropriately identify what is good and what is evil. It will also strengthen the power to exercise and translate pure and decent thoughts, and eliminate evils that allow evil thoughts to germinate and pollute the vision of the Immanent God. Referring to the universal thought-waves in terms of its torch-bearers like Buddha, Mohammed, Christ and others, Vivekananda marvellously elucidates the ends-in-view of education as follows:

Good and evil thoughts are each a potent power, and they fill the universe. As vibration continues, so thought remains in the form of thought until translated into action. For example, force is latent in the man's arm until he strikes a blow, when he translates it into activity. We are the heirs of good and evil thought. If we make ourselves pure and the instruments of good thoughts, these will enter us. The good soul will not be receptive to evil thoughts. Evil thoughts find the best field in evil people; they are like microbes which germinate and increase only when they find a suitable soil. Mere thoughts are like little wavelets; fresh impulses to vibration come to them simultaneously; until at last one great wave seems to stand up and swallow up the rest. These universal thought waves seem to recur every five hundred years, when invariably the great wave typifies and swallows up the others. It is this which constitutes a prophet. He focuses in his own mind the thought of the age in which he is living and gives it back to mankind in concrete form. Krishna, Buddha, Christ, Mohammed, and Luther may be instanced as the great waves that stood up above their fellows (with a probable lapse of five hundred years between them). Always the wave that is backed by the greatest purity and the noblest character is what breaks upon the world as a movement of social reform. Once again in our day there is a vibration of the waves of thought and the central idea is that of the Immanent God, and this is everywhere cropping up in every form and every sect. In these waves, construction alternates with destruction; yet the construction always makes an end of the work of destruction. Now as a man dives deeper to reach his spiritual nature, he feels no longer bound by superstition. The majority of sects will be transient, and last only as bubbles because the leaders are not usually men of character. Perfect love, the heart never reacting, this is what builds character. There is no allegiance possible where there is no character in the leader, and perfect purity ensures the most lasting allegiance and confidence.

—*Ibid.*, Vol. VI, pp. 134-35.

To explore and identify knowledge from an altogether new dimensions of humane development which accelerates one to have ascent and excellence from the spiritual point of view is one of the most significant contributions of Vivekananda's educational philosophy. It allows us to have a new vision of knowledge as the Bliss Absolute. He inspires everyone to follow knowledge to have a complete mastery over the senses which very often act as constraints of "living in God".

Vivekananda also considers knowledge as the perfect vehicle of making a fusion between God and man. This naturally enables one to realize that man is divine and all knowledge purified and crystallized in terms of spiritual devotion which enables one to know the true identity of the self. Knowledge thus allows one to achieve the state of the Bliss Absolute. Vivekananda unfolds this role of knowledge as a dynamic vehicle of education very adroitly:

Knowledge exists eternally. The man who discovers a spiritual truth is what we call "inspired", and what he brings to the world is revelation. But revelation too is eternal and is not to be crystallized as final and then blindly followed. Revelation may come to man who has fitted himself to receive it. Perfect purity is the most essential thing, for only "the pure in heart shall see God". Man is the highest being that exists and this is the greatest world, for here can man realize freedom. The highest concept we can have of God is man. Every attribute we give Him belongs also to man, only in a lesser degree. When we rise higher and want to get out of this concept of God, we have to get out of the body, out of mind and imagination, and leave this world out of sight. When we rise to be the absolute, we are no longer in the world—all is Subject, without object. Man is the apex of the only "world" we can ever know. Those who have attained "sameness" or perfection, are said to be "living in God". All hatred is "killing the self by the self"; therefore, love is the law of life. To rise to this is to be perfect; but the more "perfect" we are, the less work can we do. The sattvika see and know that all this world is mere child's play and do not trouble themselves about that. We are not much disturbed when we see two puppies fighting and biting each other. We know it is not a serious matter. The perfect one knows that this world is Maya. Life is called Samsara—it is the result of the conflicting forces acting upon us. ....The self is beyond both freedom and bondage. We are Brahma, we are immortal knowledge beyond the senses, we are Bliss Absolute.

—*Ibid.*, Vol. VIII, pp. 34-35.

Vivekananda explores and expands the horizon of education by means of elucidating the religion of education which is the religion of perfection. Such religion makes a harmonious marriage between feeling and understanding, where the union of head, heart and soul becomes quite affirmative and natural. As he categorically remarks:

What we want is to see the man who is harmoniously developed.....great in heart, great in mind, [great in deed]......We want the man whose heart feels intensely the miseries and sorrows of the world......And [we want] the man who not only can feel but can find the meaning of things, who delves deeply into the heart of nature and understanding. [We want] the man who will not even stop there, [but] who wants to work out [the feeling and meaning by actual deeds]. Such a combination of head, heart and hand is what we want, but you will find [that most of them] are one-sided. [One] sees the glorious midday sun of intellect [and] sees nothing else. Another hears the beautiful music of love and can hear nothing else. Another is [immersed] in activity, and has neither time to feel nor time to think. Why not [have] the giant who is equally active, equally knowing, and equally loving? Is it impossible? Certainly not. This is the man of the future, of whom there are [only a] few at present. [The number of such will increase] until the whole world is humanized.

—*Ibid.*,Vol. VI, pp. 49-50.

Delving deep into the world of knowledge, Vivekananda presents us with the real world of activity where knowledge is not bound by unexplained and confused cause and effect relationship. He always exposes it as a vehicle of a perfect fusion between cause and effect. In this fusion, he explains the role of Maya in terms of desire and non-desire. Therefore, the role of education is to have a perfect control over both desires and non-desires. As he poignantly remarks:

It is clear, therefore, that the peculiarity of all our knowledge is that it proves its own insufficiency. Again, we cannot say that it is unreal, for all the reality we know and can think of is within this knowledge. Nor can we deny that it is sufficient for all practical purposes. This state of human knowledge which celebrates within its scope both the external and the internal worlds is called Maya. It is unreal because it proves its own correctness. It is real in the sense of being sufficient for all the needs of the animal man.

Acting in the external world Maya manifests as the two powers of attraction and repulsion. In the internal its manifestations are desire and non-desire (Pravritti and Nivritti). The whole universe is trying to rush outwards. Each atom is trying to fly off from its centre. In the internal world, each thought is trying to go beyond control. Again, each particle in the external world is checked by another force, the centripetal and drawn towards the centre. Similarly, in the thought-world the controlling power is checking all these outgoing desires.

—*Ibid.*, Vol. VIII, p. 146.

To make an untiring adventure into the world of knowledge and wisdom, erudition and emancipation, is to make an eternal quest for the unknowable and the unknown, the limitable and the illimitable. Thus true education is not only to control and crystallize the senses but also to go beyond the senses. In such an adventure into the world of 'super-sensuous' the true vision of religion is effulged. As Vivekananda clearly observes:

This adventure of ours, the universe of the senses, the rational, the intellectual, is bound on both sides by the illimitable, the unknowable, the ever unknown. Herein is the search, herein are the inquiries, here are the facts; from this comes the light which is known to the world as religion. Essentially, however, religion belongs to the super-sensuous and not to the sense plane. It is beyond all reasoning, and not on the plane of intellect. It is a vision, an inspiration, a plunge into the unknown and unknowable, making the unknowable more than known, for it can never be 'known'. This search has been in the human mind, as I believe, from the very beginning of humanity. There cannot have been human reasoning and intellect in any period of the world's history without this struggle, this search beyond. In our little universe, this human mind, we see a thought arise. Whence it rises we do not know, and when it disappears, where it goes, we know not either. The macrocosm and the microcosm are, as it were, in the same groove, passing through the same stages, vibrating in the same key.

—*Ibid.*, Vol. IV, p. 203.

The education for having and cultivating the "inner light" is the key to vibrant education. For this, Vivekananda encourages everyone to be devoted to the education of love. With such education, one can ardently communicate with the heart of everyone pining for love and attention, consciousness and freedom from all forms of bondage and superstition.

Vivekananda also reminds us that the education of love for others is the only means of sacrificing the interest of the self for the greater interest of humankind. This is the surest way of winning over our petty desires, our little self and visualizing the All Beautiful in every human being. As he significantly advises:

To attain liberation through work, join yourselves to work but without desire, looking for no result. Such work leads to knowledge, which in turn brings emancipation. To give up work before you know, leads to misery. Work done for the self gives no bondage. Neither desire, pleasure nor fear pain from work. It is the mind and the body that work, not I. Tell yourself this unceasingly and realize it. Try not to know that you work.

Do all as a sacrifice to the Lord. Be in the world, but not of it, like the lotus leaf whose roots are in the mud but which remains always pure. Let your love go to all, whatever they do to you. A blind man cannot see colour, so how can we see evil unless it is in us? We compare what we see outside with what we find in ourselves and pronounce judgment accordingly. If we are pure, we cannot see impurity. It may exist, but not for us. See only God in every man, woman and child; see it by the antarjyotis, "inner light", and seeing that, we can see naught else. Do not want this world, because what you desire you get. Seek the Lord and the Lord only. The more there is, the more bondage, the more fear. How much more afraid and miserable are we than the ant! Get out of it and come to the Lord. Seek the science of the Maker and not that of the made.

—*Ibid*, Vol. VII, pp. 63-64.

The road to vibrant education as Vivekananda strongly suggests, is to explore the finer powers within everyone to be in blessed unison with the All Serene. For this, one cannot but explore one's mind ceaselessly. This will enable one to make a clear distinction between grossness and fineness till one explores the finest one—the spirit. Vivekananda directs our attention to that education which enables us to have perfect control over the mind in order to exercise purity along with that of moral and ethical values leading to religion of the right kind. As he remarkably elaborates on this point:

> There are laws, very fine, which are behind the physical law, as we know. That is to say, there are no such realities as a physical world, a mental world, a spiritual world. Whatever is, is one. Let us say, it is a sort of tapering existence, the thickest part is here; it tapers, and becomes finer and finer. The finest is what we call spirit. The grossest, the body. And just as it is here in microcosm, it is exactly the same in macrocosm. The universe of ours is exactly like that; it is the gross external thickness and it tapers into something finer and finer until it becomes God.
>
> We also know that the greatest power is lodged in the fine, not in the coarse. We see a man take up a huge weight, we see his muscles swell, and over his body we see signs of exertion, and we think that the muscles are powerful things. But it is the thin thread-like things, the nerves which bring power to the muscles; the moment one of these threads is cut off from reaching the muscles, they are not able to work at all. These tiny nerves bring the power from something still finer, and that again in its turn brings it from something finer still—thought and so on. So, it is the fine that is really the seat of power. Of course we can see the movements in the gross; but when fine movements take place, we catch it, and thus we naturally identify movements with things which are gross. But all the power is really in the fine. We do not

see any movement in the fine, perhaps, because the movement is so intense that we cannot perceive it. But if by any science, any investigation, we are helped to get hold of these finer forces which are the cause of the expression, the expression itself will be under control. There is a little bubble coming from the bottom of a lake; we do not see it coming all the time, we can see it only when it bursts on the surface; so we can perceive thoughts only after they develop a great deal or we have no control over our actions, over our thoughts. But how can we have it? If we can get control over the fine movements, if we can get hold of thought, before it has become action, then it would be possible for us to control the whole. Now, if there is a method by which we can analyze, investigate, understand, and finally grapple with those finer powers, the finer causes, then alone is it possible to have control over ourselves, and the man who has control over his own mind assuredly will have control over every other mind. That is why purity and morality have been always the object of religion; a pure, moral man has control of himself. And all minds are the same, different parts of one Mind. He who knows one lump of clay has known all the clay of the universe. He who knows and controls his own mind knows the secret of every mind and has power over every mind.

—*Ibid.*, Vol. II, pp. 16-17.

As a practical connoisseur of education, Vivekananda upholds the spirit of education primarily and most ardently as the spirit of service. That spirit of service must respond to the hapless and the hopeless, the lowliest and the lost. He, therefore, cares for dynamic and living education rooted to the head as well as to the heart. No education becomes meaningful unless it responds to the aching heart—the heart that pines for emancipation from the curse of the darkness of ignorance which does not allow anyone to manifestation of inherent personality.

Vivekananda calls upon everyone to exercise education of the highest order—the education that beckons light eternal. It is this light that responds to the yearning of the poor and the downtrodden, the despised and the ignored. It is this light, again, that prompts us to serve humankind with all responsibility and sincerity. The ultimate end-in-view of such an education is to best serve the Lord who is within every human being anywhere and everywhere.

Radical and realistic as Vivekananda is to the core of education, he introduces an altogether new dimension of education which has its universal and eternal appeal for the ascent and excellence of humankind. His clarion call to look upon everyone as God and work untiringly is the greatest lesson to be pursued with all sincerity of purpose. His own advice is very significant:

Look upon every man, woman and everyone as God. You cannot help anyone, you can only serve: serve the children of the Lord, serve the Lord Himself, if you have the privilege. If the Lord grants that you can help anyone of his children, blessed you are; do not think too much of yourselves. Blessed you are that

that privilege was given to you when others had it not. Do it only as worship. I should see God in the poor, and it is for my salvation that I go and worship them. The poor and the miserable are for our salvation, coming in the shape of the diseased, coming in the shape of the lunatic, the leper and the sinner! Bold are my words; and let me repeat that it is the greatest privilege in our life that we are allowed to serve the Lord in all these shapes. Give up the idea that by ruling over others you can do any good to them. But you can do just as much as you can in the case of the plant; you can supply the growing seed with the materials for the making up of its body, bringing to it the earth, the water, the air, that it wants. It will take all that it wants by its own nature; it will assimilate and grow by its own nature.

Bring all light into the world. Light, bring light! Let light come into everyone; the task will not be finished till everyone has reached the Lord. Bring light to the poor; and bring more light to the rich, for they require it more than the poor. Bring light to the ignorant, and more light to the educated, for the varieties of the education of our time are tremendous! Thus bring light to all and leave the rest unto the Lord, for in the words of the same Lord, "To work you have the right and not to the fruits thereof."

—*Ibid.*, Vol. III, pp. 246-47.

The education that Vivekananda considers apposite for a vibrant society is to select an ideal best suited to the well-being of everyone. Not utilitarianism but altruism now and for ever is the lesson which should serve as the guiding force of education for social advancement. He, therefore, unfolds the appalling limitations of utilitarianism that affects the very backbone of any society:

> Any system that wants to bind men down to the limits of their own societies is not able to find an explanation for the ethical laws of mankind. The utilitarian wants us to give up the struggle after the Infinite, the reaching-out for the Super-sensuous, as impracticable as absurd, and in the same breath asks us to take up ethics and do good to the society. Why should we do good? Doing good is a secondary consideration. We must have an ideal. Ethics itself is not the end, but the means to the end. If the end is not there, why should we be ethical? Why should I do good to the other men, and not injure them? If happiness is the good of mankind why should I not make myself happy and others unhappy? What prevents me? In the second place, the basis of utility is too narrow. All the current social forms and methods are derived from society as it exists, but what right has the Utilitarian to assume that society is eternal? Society did not exist ages ago, possibly will not exist ages hence. Most probably, it is one of the passing stages through which we are going towards a higher evolution, and any law that is derived from society alone cannot be eternal, cannot cover the whole ground of man's nature. At best, therefore, utilitarian theories can only work under present social conditions. Beyond that they have no value.
>
> —*Ibid.*, Vol. II, pp. 63-64.

The education for an enlightened society necessitates cohesion between life and work. It also demands self-sacrifice of the highest order. Vivekananda, of course, demands a greater involvement where compromise with cowardice has no room at all in any form whatsoever. The lesson of universal love through education is what brings forth worthy dividends in every sphere of life. Defining and explaining the true role of education, he adroitly remarks:

What is education? Is it book-learning? No. Is it diverse knowledge? Not even that. The training by which the current and expression of will are brought under control and become fruitful is called education. Now consider, is that education as a result of which the will, being continually choked by force through generations, is well-nigh killed out; is that education under whose sway even the old ideas, let alone the new ones, are disappearing one by one; is that education which is slowly making a man machine? It is more blessed, in my opinion, even to go wrong, impelled by one's free will and intelligence than to be good as an automation. Again, can that be called society which is formed by an aggregate of men who are like lumps of clay, like lifeless machines, like heaped up pebbles? How can such society fare well? Were good possible, then instead of being slaves for hundreds of years, we would have been he greatest nation on earth, and this soil of India, instead of being a mine of stupidity, would have been the eternal fountain-head of learning. Is not self-sacrifice, then, a virtue? Is it not the most virtuous deed to sacrifice the happiness of one, the welfare of one, for the sake of the many? Exactly, but as the Bengali adage goes, "Can beauty be manufactured by rubbing and scrubbing? Can love be generated by effort and compulsion?" what glory is there in the renunciation of an eternal beggar? What virtue is there in the sense-control of one devoid of sense-power? What again is the self-sacrifice of one devoid of idea, devoid of heart, devoid of high ambition, and devoid of the conception of what constitutes society?

—*Ibid.*, Vol. IV, pp. 490-91.

Moreover, Vivekananda goes to the length of criticizing parents promoting education for self-interest and dwarfing the inherent spirit of universal love to be untiringly cultivated by their children:

The truth is that in this country parents and relations can ruthlessly sacrifice the best interests of their children and others for their own selfish ends to save themselves by compromise to society; and the teaching of generations rendering the mind callous has made it perfectly easy. He, the brave alone, can deny self. The coward, afraid of the lash, with one hand wipes his eyes and gives with the other. Of what avail are such gifts? It is a far cry to love universal. The young plant should be hedged in and taken care of. One can hope gradually to attain to universal love if one can learn to love one object unselfishly. If devotion to one particular Ishta Deva is attained, devotion to universal Virat is gradually possible.

—*Ibid.*, p. 491.

To keep pace with the progress of time along with the progress of the learner should always be taken into serious consideration in imparting education. Explore the learner and teach accordingly is the only means of success in learning and teaching. The teacher who has the incomparable ability to make an inspiring and thrilling entry into the learner's attitude and interest in learning wins half the battle as it were of teaching.

To present before the learner a 'whole museum of truths', as Vivekananda suggests, is to invite him/her into a world of adventure where he/she moulds, modifies or translates his/her own vision in the light of truth. As regards harmonious development through education, Vivekananda's viewpoints are eternally relevant:

Time is merely the measures of our thoughts, and thought being inconceivably swift, there is no limit to the speed with which we can live the life ahead. So it cannot be stated how long it would take to live all future life. It might be in a second, or it might take fifty lifetimes. It depends on the intensity of the desire. The teaching must therefore be modified according to the needs of the taught. The consuming fire is ready for all, even water and chunks of ice quickly consume. Fire a mass of bird-shot, one at least will strike; give a man a whole museum of truths, he will at once take what is suited to him. Past lives have moulded our tendencies; give to the taught in accordance with his tendency. Intellectual, mystical, devotional, practical—make one the basis, but teach the others with it. Intellect must be balanced with love, the mystical nature with reason, while practice must form part of every method. Take everyone where he stands and push him forward. Religious teaching must always be constructive, not destructive.

Each tendency shows the life-work of the past, the line or radius along which that man must move. All radii lead to the centre. Never even attempt to disturb anyone's tendencies; to do that puts back both teacher and taught. When you teach Jnana, you must become a Jnani and stand mentally exactly where the taught stands. Similarly, in every other Joga. Develop every faculty as if it were the only one possessed, this is the true secret of so-called harmonious development. That is, get exactly with intensity, but not at its expense. We are infinite. There is no limitation in us, we can be as intense as the most devoted Mohammedan and as broad as the roaring atheist.

The way to do this is not to put the mind on any one subject, but to develop and control the mind itself; then you can turn it on any side you choose. Thus you keep the intensity and extensity. Feel Jnana as if it were all there was, then do the same with Bhakti, with Raja (Yoga), with Karma. Give up the waves and go to the ocean, then you can have the waves as you please. Control the "lake" of your own mind, else you cannot understand the lake of another's mind.

—*Ibid.*, Vol. VII, pp. 97-99.

What, then, should be the role of a teacher? What should be the true teacher's strategies for imparting education of the best kind for acceptance and acceleration of the best mind? Here is Vivekananda's explicit answer:

> The true teacher is one who can throw his whole force into the tendency of the taught. Without real sympathy we can never teach well. Give up the notion that man is a responsible being, only the perfect man is responsible. The ignorant have drunk deep of the cup of delusion and are not sane. You, who know, must have infinite patience with these. Have nothing but love for them and find out the disease that has made them see the world in a wrong light, then help them to cure it and aright. Remember always that only the free can have free will, all the rest are in bondage and are not responsible for what they do. Will as will is bound. The water when melting on the top of the Himalayas is free, but becoming the river, it is bound by the banks; yet the original impetus carries it to the sea, and it regains its freedom. The first one is the "fall of man", the second is the "resurrection". Not one can rest until it finds its freedom.
>
> —*Ibid.*, p. 99.

The education of proper exercise of freedom is certainly not easy. But what is more difficult is the education of patience. Unless patience is not learnt and exercised in all experience in every walk of life, education loses one of its fundamental objectives and becomes meaningless and useless. What is greatly needed is not merely acquisition of knowledge but dissemination of knowledge everywhere without making an inane, unfortunate, sordid and shameful distinction between the high and the low, the rich and the poor, the wise and the ignorant and so on. True education never allows any such distinction under any circumstances.

Vivekananda reminds us that the education of patience and freedom is the pathfinder to perfection. And, for this, work, relentless work is the touchstone. In his own words:

There will be less of fanaticism and more of real work. Fanatics cannot work; they waste three-fourths of their energy. It is the level-headed, calm, practical man who works. So, the power to work will increase from this idea. Knowing that this is the state of things, there will be more patience. The sight of misery or of evil will not be able to throw us off our balance and make us run after shadows. Therefore, patience will come to us, knowing that the world will have to go on in its own way. If, for instance, all men have become good, the animals will have in the meantime evolved into men, and will have to pass through the same state, and so with the plants. But only one thing is certain; the mighty river is rushing towards the ocean, and all the drops that constitute the stream will in time be drawn into that boundless ocean. So, in this life, with all its miseries, and sorrows, its joys and smiles and tears, one thing is certain, that all things are rushing towards their goal, and it is only a question of time when you and I, and plants and animals, and every particle of life that exists must reach the Infinite Ocean of Perfection, must attain to Freedom, to God.

—*Ibid.*, Vol. II, pp. 101-02.

The knowledge of One in order to eliminate the distinction between I and we, the knowledge of oneness with everyone is the essential end-in-view of living education. Vivekananda wants that purity and perfection of knowledge leading to living education. Why does he think so? Why does he want to give priority to that education where 'I' is merged in 'we' and vice versa? The answer is clear and simple, and, therefore, ardently and extremely desirable, because the best outcome of education is obviously extinction of personality.

At the same time, education cares for that knowledge which shows the way of how to make an endless adventure into the world of truth. This world will certainly direct one to think and act selflessly for the cause of others. Thus one loves to deny the self for the well-being of others. This spirit of altruism is the spirit of identifying oneself with God—the spirit which can only be ignited by means of true education. In this connection Vivekananda's characteristic interpretation deserves our serious attention:

"Know the truth and be free in a moment." All the darkness will then vanish. When man has seen himself as one with the Infinite Being of the universe, when all separateness is ceased, when all men and women, all gods and angels, all animals and plants, and the whole universe have melted into that Oneness, the all fear disappears. Can I hurt myself? Can I kill myself? Can I injure myself? Whom to fear! Can you fear yourself? Then will all sorrow disappear. What can cause me sorrow? I am the one Existence of the universe. Then all jealousies will disappear; of whom to be jealous? Of myself? Then all bad feelings disappear. Against whom can I have bad feeling? Against myself? There is none in the universe but I. and this is the one way, says the Vedanta, to Knowledge. Kill out this differentiation, kill out this superstition that there are many. "He who in this world of many sees the One, he who in this mass of insentiency sees the one Sentient Being, he who in this world of shadows catches that Reality, unto him belongs eternal peace, unto none else, unto none else."

Why is it that everyone says, "Do good to others?" where is the explanation? Why is it that all great men have preached the brotherhood of mankind, and greater men the brotherhood of all lives? Because whether they were conscious of it or not, behind all that, through all their irrational and personal superstitions, was peering forth the eternal light of the self denying all manifoldness, and assuring that the whole universe is but one.

Again, the last word gave us one universe, which through the senses we see as matter, through the intellect as souls, and through the spirit as God. To the man who throws upon himself veils, which the world calls wickedness and evil, this very universe will change and become a hideous place; to another man, who wants enjoyments, this very universe will change its appearance and become a heaven, and to the perfect man the whole thing will vanish and become his own self.

Injure none, deny the position of none; take man where he stands and, if you can, lend him a helping hand and put him on a higher platform, but do not injure and do not destroy. All will come to truth in the long run. "When all the desires of the heart will be vanquished, this very mortal will become immortal"—then the very man will become God.

—*Ibid.*, pp. 251-53.

The education of love, as Vivekananda exposes, is the hallmark of vibrant and living education. Highest knowledge is the outcome of extreme love crystallized in terms of sincerity and devotion, impartiality and adoration of all forms of goodness and truth leading to the ascent of man.

Vivekananda invites us to pursue the education of love with all naturalness and abiding faith in the divinity of man. As he advocates the concept of love in terms of knowledge:

"Love is higher than work, than Yoga, than knowledge."

Work is merely a schooling for the doer; it can do no good to others. We must work out our own problem; the prophets only show us how to work, "What you think, you become", so if you throw your burden on Jesus, you will have to think of Him and thus become like Him—you love Him.

"Extreme love and highest knowledge are one."

But theorizing about God will not do; we must love and work. Give up the world and all worldly things, especially when the "plant" is tender. Day and night think of God and think of nothing else as far as possible. The daily necessary thoughts can all be brought through God. Eat to Him, drink to Him, sleep to Him, see Him in all. Talk of God to others; this is most beneficial.

Get the mercy of God and of His greatest children; these are the two chief ways to God, the company of these children of light is very hard to get; five minutes in their company will change a whole life; and if you really want it enough, one will come to you. The presence of those who love God makes a place holy, "such is the glory of the children of the Lord." They are He, and when they speak, their words are scriptures. The place where they have been becomes filled with their vibrations, and those going there feel them and have a tendency to become holy also.

"To such lovers there is no distinction of caste, learning, beauty, birth, wealth, or occupation; because all are His."

Give up all evil company, especially at the beginning. Avoid worldly company that will distract your mind. Give up all "me and mine". To him who has nothing in the universe the Lord comes. Cut the bondage of all worldly affections; go beyond laziness and all care as to what becomes of you. Never turn back to see the result of what you have done. Give all to the Lord and go on and think not of it. The whole soul pours in a continuous current to God; there is no time to seek money, or name, or fame, no time to think of anything but God; then will come into our hearts that infinite, wonderful bliss of Love. All desires are but beads of glass. Love of God increases every moment and is ever new, to be known only by feeling it. Love is the easiest of all, it waits for no logic, it is natural. We need no demonstration, no proof. Reasoning is limiting something by our own minds. We throw a net and catch something, and they say that we have demonstrated it; but never, never can we catch God in a net.

Love should be unrelated. Even when we love wrongly, it is of the true love, of the true bliss; the power is the same, use it as we may. Its very nature is peace and bliss. The murderer when he kisses his baby forgets for an instant all but love. Give up all self, all egotism; get out of anger, lust, give all to God. "I am not, but Thou art; the old man is all gone, only Thou remained." "I am Thou." Blame none; if evil comes, know the Lord is playing with you and be exceeding[ly] glad.

Love is beyond time and space, it is absolute.

—*Ibid.*, Vol. VII, pp. 9-11.

Apart from the education of love that shows one the right road to fullness of education, Vivekananda advocates education as an inherent evolution of man as God. The external matters in forms of constraints, obstacles, calamities, ukase whatsoever can never tarnish the image of God within man. What is required is the lesson of steadfastness to uphold and enrich the All Serene within so that extinction from all impediments becomes a natural efflorescence of personality.

Substantiating the view as above, Vivekananda refines the role of education where competition is alien to the history of excellence and ascent of man. Simultaneously, competition acts as a blob to the evolution of man as God. Evolution is independent and indifferent to any external force, and the history of man should, from this genuine point of view, be written anew and afresh. Moreover, the great lesson that we receive from true education is: we should never be competitive amongst ourselves. Who competes, and with whom? The struggle that beckons us is always to be done alone and should never call forth others' assistance. Therein lies the efflorescence of education we strive for and cultivate for excellence. That also signifies purity and perfection of strength of mind and character.

Admittedly, Vivekananda unfolds a newer avenue of education for advancement where all the components as above have been extraordinarily dealt with apposite perspectives. As he remarkably spells out:

Our education and progression simply mean taking away the obstacles, and by its own nature the divinity will manifest itself. This does away with all the struggle for existence. The miserable experiences are simply in the way, and can be eliminated entirely. They are not necessary for evolution. Even if they did not exist, we should progress. It is in the very nature of things to manifest themselves. The momentum is not from outside, but comes from inside. Each soul is the sum total of the universal experience already coiled up there; and of all these experiences, only those will come out which find suitable circumstances.

So the external things can only give us environments. These competitions and struggles and evils that we see are not the effect of the involution or the cause but they are in the way. If they did not exist, still man would go on and evolve as God, because it is the very nature of that God to come out and manifest Himself. To my mind, this seems very hopeful, instead of that horrible idea of competition. The more I study history, the more I find that idea to be wrong. Some say that if man did not fight with man, he would not progress. I also used to think so, but I find now that every war has thrown back human progress by fifty years instead of hurrying it forwards. The day will come when men will study history from a different light and find that competition is neither the cause, nor the effect, simply a thing on the way, not necessary to evolution at all.

The most horrible thing about competition is that one may conquer the environments, but that where one may conquer, thousands are crowded out. So it is evil at best. That cannot be good which helps only one and hinders the majority. Patanjali says that these struggles remain only through our ignorance, and are not necessary, and we are not part of the evolution of man. It is just our impatience which creates them. We have not the patience to go and work our way out. For instance, there is a fire in a theatre, and only a few escape. The rest in trying to rush out crush one another down. That crush was not necessary for the salvation of the building nor of the two or three who escaped. If all had gone out slowly, not one would have been hurt. That is the case in life. The doors are open for us, and we can all get out without the competition and struggle; and yet we struggle. The struggle we create through our own ignorance, through impatience; we are in too great a hurry. The highest manifestation of strength is to keep ourselves calm and on our own feet.

—*Ibid.*, Vol. V, pp. 277-79.

Education always cares for union of minds and never allows man to be dissociated from man. It proclaims and fosters the spirit of oneness. The knowledge that we receive through education of the right mind always allows freedom and truth to be manifested at one's own will. What type of freedom and truth should one nurse? What type of self-assessment should be made? To pursue freedom and truth in the light of education is to realize oneself in terms of the spirit of God within and act accordingly. Therefore, the spiritual serenity of human action always serves as a shield for one's ascent and excellence and liberation from ignorance. In the invaluable words of Vivekananda:

Many want pleasure [as] the goal. For that pleasure they seek only the senses. On the higher planes much pleasure is to be sought. Then on spiritual planes. Then in himself—God within him.

The man whose pleasure is outside of [himself] becomes unhappy when that outside thing goes. You cannot depend for this pleasure upon anything in this universe. If all my pleasures are in myself, I must have pleasure all the time because I can never lose my Self....Mother, father, child, wife, body, wealth—everything I can lose except my self....bliss in the Self. All desire is contained in the Self....This is individuality which never changes, and this is perfect.

....And how to get it? They find what the great souls of this world—all great men and women found [through sustained discrimination]....What of these dualistic theories of twenty gods, thirty gods? It does not matter. They all had the one truth, that this false individuality must go....So this ego——the less there is of it, the nearer I am to that which I really am: the universal body. The less I think of my own individual mind, the nearer I am to that universal mind. The less I think of my own soul, the nearer I am to that universal soul.

—*Ibid*, Vol. II, pp. 468—469.

Elimination of the self for the greater cause of the universal self is the key to excellence of education for which Vivekananda always advocates. This teaches the lesson of how to be truly educated and rise above selfishness. This also paves path to the fusion of 'I' and 'thou' and highlights universalism through education of the right mind. The mind thus prepared for the lesson of altruism enables a learner to exercise emotional sensibilities and finer visions of life for the welfare of the entire humankind. Vivekananda remarkably spells out this essential end-in-view of education in the following invaluable words:

> Just as this universe has its existence in separation, in distinction, and all the while is rushing towards unity, non-separation, so in our little worlds each soul is born, as it were, cut off from the rest of the world. The more ignorant, the more unenlightened the soul, the more it thinks that it is separate from the rest of the universe. The more ignorant the person, the more he thinks, he will die or will be born, and so forth—ideas that are an expression of this separateness. But we find that, as knowledge comes, man grows, morality is evolved, and the idea of non-separateness begins. Whether men understand it or not, they are impelled by that power behind to become unselfish. This is the foundation of all morality. It is the quintessence of all ethics, preached in any language, or in any religion, or by any prophet in the world "Be thou unselfish", "Not I", but "thou"—that is the background of all ethical codes. And what is meant by this is the recognition of non-individuality—that you are a part of me, and I of you; the recognition that in hurting you I hurt myself, and in helping you I help myself; the recognition that there cannot possibly be death for me when you live. When one worm lives in this universe, how can I die? For my life is in the life of that worm. At the same time it will teach me that we can leave one of our fellow-beings without helping him, that in his good consists my good.
>
> —*Ibid.*, Vol. VI, pp. 5-6.

Elsewhere, Vivekananda, while explaining the avenue of self-realisation, takes recourse to the spirit of doing good to others which also ensures realization of God:

> We become forgetful of the ego when we think of the body as dedicated to the service of others—the body with which most complacently we identify the ego. And in the long run comes the consciousness of disembodiedness. The more intently you think of the well-being of others, the more oblivious of self you become. In this way, as gradually your heart gets purified by work, you will come to feel the truth that your own Self is pervading all beings and all things. Thus it is that doing good to others constitutes a way, a means of revealing one's own Self or Atman. Know this also to be one of the spiritual practices, discipline for God-realisation.
>
> —*Ibid.*, Vol. VII, pp.111-112.

The education that one seeks through devotion should always be guided by this spirit of the love for goodness which truly indicates the path of renunciation. The education of love is the spirit that pervades in the entire living beings. It teaches the great lesson of cohesion and enunciation leading one to eliminate personal interests and preparing one, through Bhakti-Yoga, to be christened with real or higher love that manifests the All Serene as Love. As Vivekananda adroitly elucidates:

> We see love everywhere in nature. Whatever in society is good and great and sublime is the working

out of that love; whatever in society is very bad, nay diabolical, is also the ill-directed working out of the same emotion of love. It is this same emotion that gives us the pure and holy conjugal love between husband and wife as well as the sort of love that goes to satisfy the lowest forms of animal passion. The emotion is the same, but its manifestation is different in different cases. It is the same feeling of love well or ill directed, that impels one man to do good and to give all he has to the poor, while it makes another man cut the throats of his brethren and take away all their possessions. The former loves others as much as the latter loves himself. The direction of the love is bad in the case of the latter, but it is right and proper in the other case. The same fire that cooks a meal for us may burn a child, and it is no fault of the fire if it does so; the difference lies in the way in which it is used. Therefore love, intense longing for association, the strong desire on the part of two to become one—and it may be, after all, of all to become merged in one—is being manifested everywhere in higher or lower forms as the case may be.

Bhakti-Yoga is the science of higher love. It shows us how to direct it; it shows us how to control it, how to manage it, how to use it, how to give it a new aim, as it were, and from it obtain the highest and most glorious results, that is, how to make it lead us to spiritual blessedness. Bhakti-Yoga does not say, "Give up"; it only says, "Love; love the Highest!"—and everything low naturally falls off from him, the object of whose love is the Highest.

—*Ibid.*, Vol. III, pp. 73-74.

The role of religion in education is very often misunderstood or misinterpreted. That the religion of education is based on the education of religion is very often ignored in our evaluation of both education and religion. Their inseparable identity for the ascent of mankind is what Vivekananda time and again points out on various occasions. While spelling out knowledge in terms of reason and religion, he highlights religion as the supreme knowledge which always makes room for scientific reasoning. He does not allow knowledge to be nurtured in ambiguity or irrationality. True religion always serves knowledge as a guiding spirit of the infinite—the spirit that enjoys the warmth of divinity. As he characteristically asserts:

Religions have been again ad again defeated, and almost exterminated. The worship of the goddess of Reason during the French Revolution was not the first manifestation of that phenomenon in the history of humanity, it was a re-enactment of what had happened in ancient times, but in modern times it has assumed greater proportions. The physical sciences are better equipped now than formerly, and religions have become less and less equipped. The foundations have been all undermined, and the modern man, whatever he may say in public, knows in the privacy of his heart that he can no more "believe". Believing certain things because an organized body of priests tells him to believe, believing because his people like him to believe, the modern man knows to be impossible for him. There are, of course, a number of people who seem to acquiesce in the so-called popular faith, but we also know for certain that they do not think. Their idea of belief may be better translated as "not-thinking-carelessness". This fight cannot last much longer without breaking to pieces all the buildings of religion.

The question is: Is there a way out? To put it in a more concrete form: Is religion to justify itself by the discoveries of reason, through which every other science justifies itself? Are the same methods of investigation, which we apply to sciences and knowledge outside, to be applied to the science of Religion? In my opinion this must be so, and I am also of opinion that the sooner it is done the better. If a religion is destroyed by such investigations, it was then all the time useless, unworthy superstition; and the sooner it goes the better. I am thoroughly convinced that its destruction would be the best thing that could happen. All that is dross would be taken off, no doubt, but the essential parts of religion will emerge triumphant out of this investigation. Not only will it be made scientific—as scientific, at least, as any of the conclusions of physics or chemistry—but will have greater strength, because physics or chemistry has no internal mandate to vouch for its truth, which religion has.

—*Ibid.*, Vol. I, pp. 366-367.

A broadened vision and a widened outlook in understanding and practising religion is the highest and noblest strategy of how to have the apposite education of religion. There is never any room for narrowness or selfish attitude in the sphere of exercising religion in right earnest. Liberalism is the only way out to explore and expand the canvas of mutual understanding and appreciation to different religions. Love for and learning the essence of every religion are the touchstones of religious altruism. Vivekananda characteristically exposes this very important lesson on the education of religious learning and teaching:

> If God wished that people should follow one religion, why have so many religions sprung up? Methods have been vainly tried to force one religion upon everyone. Even when the sword was lifted to make all people to follow one religion, history tells us that ten religions sprang up in its place. One religion cannot suit all. Man is the product of two forces, action and reaction, which make him think. If such forces did not exercise a man's mind, he would be incapable of thinking. Man is a creature who thinks; Manushya (man) is a being with Manas (mind); and as soon as his thinking power goes, he becomes no better than an animal. Who would like such a man? God forbid that any such state should come upon the people of India. Variety in unity is necessary to keep man as man. Variety ought to be preserved in everything; for as long as there is variety the world will exist. Of course variety does not mean that one is small and the other is great; but if all play their parts equally well in their respective position in life, the variety is still preserved. In every religion there have been men good and able, thus making the religion to which they belonged worthy of respect; and as there are such people in every religion, there ought to be no hatred for any sect whatsoever.
>
> —*Ibid.*, Vol. III, pp. 359-360.

The education of altruism in and through religion as Vivekananda points out is always a guide to explore the divinity of man in terms of love. To love man is to love God. But that love must be an outcome of the lesson of extinction of personality. There is no room for personal gain. Nor is there any scope for exhibitionism whatsoever or howsoever under any circumstances. The true education of religion does not teach any lesson of bargaining. Vivekananda's elucidation on this point is very significant:

> Love we hear spoken of everywhere. Everyone says, "Love God." Men do not know what is to love; if they did, they would not talk so glibly about it. Every man says he can love, and then, in no time, finds out that there is no love in his nature. Every woman says she can love and soon finds out that she cannot. The world is full of the talk of love, but it is hard to love. Where is love? How do you know that there is love? The first test of love is that it knows no bargaining. So long as you see a man love another only to get something from him, you know that that is not love; it is shop-keeping. Wherever there is any question of buying and selling, it is not love. So, when a man prays to God, "Give me this, and give me that", it is not love. How can it be? I offer you a prayer, and you give me something in return; that is what it is, mere shop-keeping.
>
> —*Ibid.*, Vol. II, p. 47.

Vivekananda also expands the horizon of education for transparency and transcendence. For this, his vision of education unfolds a superior canvas of ascent for humankind. What he speaks on Jnana-Yoga clearly spells out his philosophy of the ascent of man in terms of education:

First, meditation should be of a negative nature. Think away everything. Analyse everything that comes in the mind by the sheer action of the will.

Next, assert what we really are—existence, knowledge and bliss—being, knowing, and loving.

Meditation is the means of unification of the subject and the object. Meditate:

Above, it is full of me; below it is full of me; in the middle, it is full of me. I am in all beings, and all beings are in me. Om Tat Sat, I am It. I am existence above mind. I am the one Spirit of the universe. I am neither pleasure nor pain.

The body, drinks, eats, and so on. I am not the body. I am not mind. I am He.

I am the witness. I look on. When health comes I am the witness. When disease comes I am the witness.

I am Existence, Knowledge, Bliss.

I am the essence and nectar of knowledge. Through eternity I change not. I am calm, resplendent, and unchanging.

—*Ibid.*, Vol. VI, pp. 91-92.

Vivekananda has heightened education to that state where man finds a new status, a rare honour of humanism embodied in the spirit of divinity. Such a state blesses us with the greatest gifts of education: self-evaluation and self-advancement in highest realities and realisations. In his own introspective words:

> Tossed to and fro, from wave to wave
>
> in this soothing, surging sea
>
> Of passions strong and sorrows deep,
>
> grief is, and joy to be,
>
> Where life is living death, alas!
>
> and death—who knows but 'tis
>
> Another start, another round of this old wheel
>
> of grief and bliss?
>
> Where children dream bright, golden dreams,
>
> too soon to find them dust,
>
> And aye look back to hope long lost
>
> and life a mass of rust!
>
> Too late, the knowledge age doth gain;
>
> scarce from the wheel we're gone
>
> When fresh, young lives put their strength
>
> to the wheel, which thus goes on
>
> From day to day and year to year.

'Tis but delusion's toy,

False hope its motor; desire, nave;

its spokes are grief and joy.

—*Ibid.*, p. 176.

For Vivekananda, there is nothing stronger than education for the well-being of humanity. When would we respond with all eagerness and courage of conviction?

Index